MznLnx

Missing Links Exam Preps

Exam Prep for

Short-Term Financial Management

Maness & Zietlow, 3rd Edition

The MznLnx Exam Prep is your link from the texbook and lecture to your exams.
The MznLnx Exam Preps are unauthorized and comprehensive reviews of your textbooks.

All material provided by MznLnx and Rico Publications (c) 2010
Textbook publishers and textbook authors do not particpate in or contribute to these reviews.

MznLnx

Rico Publications

Exam Prep for Short-Term Financial Management
3rd Edition
Maness & Zietlow

Publisher: Raymond Houge
Assistant Editor: Michael Rouger
Text and Cover Designer: Lisa Buckner
Marketing Manager: Sara Swagger
Project Manager, Editorial Production: Jerry Emerson
Art Director: Vernon Lowerui

Product Manager: Dave Mason
Editorial Assitant: Rachel Guzmanji
Pedagogy: Debra Long
Cover Image: Jim Reed/Getty Images
Text and Cover Printer: City Printing, Inc.
Compositor: Media Mix, Inc.

(c) 2010 Rico Publications

ALL RIGHTS RESERVED. No part of this work covered by the copyright may be reproduced or used in any form or by an means--graphic, electronic, or mechanical, including photocopying, recording, taping, Web distribution, information storage, and retrieval systems, or in any other manner--without the written permission of the publisher.

Printed in the United States
ISBN:

For more information about our products, contact us at:
Dave.Mason@RicoPublications.com

For permission to use material from this text or product, submit a request online to:
Dave.Mason@RicoPublications.com

Contents

CHAPTER 1
The Role of Working Capital — 1

CHAPTER 2
Analysis of Solvency, Liquidity, and Financial Flexibility — 5

CHAPTER 3
Valuation — 8

CHAPTER 4
Inventory Management — 15

CHAPTER 5
Accounts Receivable Management — 20

CHAPTER 6
Credit Policy and Collections — 23

CHAPTER 7
Managing Payables and Accruals — 27

CHAPTER 8
The Payment System and Financial Institution Relationships — 31

CHAPTER 9
Cash Collection Systems — 39

CHAPTER 10
Cash Concentration — 43

CHAPTER 11
Cash Disbursement Systems — 46

CHAPTER 12
Cash Forecasting — 51

CHAPTER 13
Short-Term Financial Planning — 58

CHAPTER 14
The Money Market — 60

CHAPTER 15
Short-Term Investment Management — 69

CHAPTER 16
Short-Term Financing — 75

CHAPTER 17
Managing Multinational Cash Flows — 82

CHAPTER 18
Managing Financial Risk With Derivatives — 87

CHAPTER 19
Treasury Information Management — 93

ANSWER KEY — 100

TO THE STUDENT

COMPREHENSIVE

The *MznLnx* Exam Prep series is designed to help you pass your exams. Editors at MznLnx review your textbooks and then prepare these practice exams to help you master the textbook material. Unlike study guides, workbooks, and practice tests provided by the texbook publisher and textbook authors, *MznLnx* gives you **all** of the material in each chapter in exam form, not just samples, so you can be sure to nail your exam.

MECHANICAL

The MznLnx Exam Prep series creates exams that will help you learn the subject matter as well as test you on your understanding. Each question is designed to help you master the concept. Just working through the exams, you gain an understanding of the subject--its a simple mechanical process that produces success.

INTEGRATED STUDY GUIDE AND REVIEW

MznLnx is not just a set of exams designed to test you, its also a comprehensive review of the subject content. Each exam question is also a review of the concept, making sure that you will get the answer correct without having to go to other sources of material. You learn as you go! Its the easiest way to pass an exam.

HUMOR

Studying can be tedious and dry. MznLnx's instructional design includes moderate humor within the exam questions on occassion, to break the tedium and revitalize the brain

Chapter 1. The Role of Working Capital

1. _____ is the balance of the amounts of cash being received and paid by a business during a defined period of time, sometimes tied to a specific project. Measurement of _____ can be used

   - to evaluate the state or performance of a business or project.
   - to determine problems with liquidity. Being profitable does not necessarily mean being liquid. A company can fail because of a shortage of cash, even while profitable.
   - to generate project rate of returns. The time of _____s into and out of projects are used as inputs to financial models such as internal rate of return, and net present value.
   - to examine income or growth of a business when it is believed that accrual accounting concepts do not represent economic realities. Alternately, _____ can be used to 'validate' the net income generated by accrual accounting.

   _____ as a generic term may be used differently depending on context, and certain _____ definitions may be adapted by analysts and users for their own uses. Common terms include operating _____ and free _____.

   _____s can be classified into:

   1. Operational _____s: Cash received or expended as a result of the company's core business activities.
   2. Investment _____s: Cash received or expended through capital expenditure, investments or acquisitions.
   3. Financing _____s: Cash received or expended as a result of financial activities, such as interests and dividends.

   All three together - the net _____ - are necessary to reconcile the beginning cash balance to the ending cash balance. Loan draw downs or equity injections, that is just shifting of capital but no expenditure as such, are not considered in the net _____.

   a. Corporate finance
   c. Cash flow
   b. Real option
   d. Shareholder value

2. A _____ is a business that pursues payments on debts owed by individuals or businesses. Most collection agencies operate as agents of creditors and collect debts for a fee or percentage of the total amount owed. Some agencies, sometimes referred to as 'debt buyers', purchase debts from creditors for a fraction of the value of the debt and pursue the debtor for the full balance.
   a. Partial Payment
   c. Commercial hard money
   b. Guaranteed consumer funding
   d. Collection agency

3. The free _____ of a public company is an estimate of the proportion of shares that are not held by large owners and that are not stock with sales restrictions (restricted stock that cannot be sold until they become unrestricted stock.)

Chapter 1. The Role of Working Capital

The free _____ or a public _____ is usually defined as being all shares held by investors other than:

- shares held by owners owning more than 5% of all shares (those could be institutional investors, 'strategic shareholders,' founders, executives, and other insiders' holdings)
- restricted stocks (granted to executives that can be, but don't have to be, registered insiders)
- insider holdings (it is assumed that insiders hold stock for the very long term)

The free _____ is an important criterion in quoting a share on the stock market.

To _____ a company means to list its shares on a public stock exchange through an initial public offering (or 'flotation'.)

- Open market
- Outstanding shares
- Market capitalization
- Public _____ loat
- Reverse takeover

a. Golden parachute
b. Trade finance
c. Float
d. Synthetic CDO

4. _____ is the difference between price and the costs of bringing to market whatever it is that is accounted as an enterprise (whether by harvest, extraction, manufacture, or purchase) in terms of the component costs of delivered goods and/or services and any operating or other expenses.

A key difficulty in measuring profit is in defining costs. Pure economic monetary profits can be zero or negative even in competitive equilibrium when accounted monetized costs exceed monetized price.

a. Accounting profit
b. Economic profit
c. AAB
d. A Random Walk Down Wall Street

5. _____ is a list for goods and materials held available in stock by a business. It is also used for a list of the contents of a household and for a list for testamentary purposes of the possessions of someone who has died. In accounting _____ is considered an asset.

a. ABN Amro
b. Inventory
c. AAB
d. A Random Walk Down Wall Street

6. The institution most often referenced by the word '_____' is a public or publicly traded _____, the shares of which are traded on a public stock exchange (e.g., the New York Stock Exchange or Nasdaq in the United States) where shares of stock of _____s are bought and sold by and to the general public. Most of the largest businesses in the world are publicly traded _____s. However, the majority of _____s are said to be closely held, privately held or close _____s, meaning that no ready market exists for the trading of shares.

a. Protect
b. Federal Home Loan Mortgage Corporation
c. Depository Trust Company
d. Corporation

7. _____, consists of the buying and selling of products or services over electronic systems such as the Internet and other computer networks. The amount of trade conducted electronically has grown extraordinarily with widespread Internet usage. The use of commerce is conducted in this way, spurring and drawing on innovations in electronic funds transfer, supply chain management, Internet marketing, online transaction processing, electronic data interchange (EDI), inventory management systems, and automated data collection systems.
a. AAB
b. ABN Amro
c. A Random Walk Down Wall Street
d. Electronic commerce

8. _____ is an inventory strategy implemented to improve the return on investment of a business by reducing in-process inventory and its associated carrying costs. In order to achieve _____ the process must have signals of what is going on elsewhere within the process. This means that the process is often driven by a series of signals, which can be Kanban, that tell production processes when to make the next part.
a. Debtor-in-possession financing
b. Pac-Man defense
c. Greed and fear
d. Just-in-time

9. _____ is a financial metric which represents operating liquidity available to a business. Along with fixed assets such as plant and equipment, _____ is considered a part of operating capital. It is calculated as current assets minus current liabilities.
a. Working Capital
b. 529 plan
c. Working capital management
d. 4-4-5 Calendar

10. _____, in bookkeeping, refers to assets, liabilities, income, and expenses recorded on individual pages of the so called book of final entry or ledger. Changes in _____ value are made by chronologically posting debit (DR) and credit (CR) entries to its page. Examples of _____s are cash, _____s receivable, mortgages, loans, land and buildings, common stock, sales, services provided, wages, and payroll overhead.
a. Accretion
b. Option
c. Alpha
d. Account

11. _____ is a file or account that contains money that a person or company owes to suppliers, but hasn't paid yet (a form of debt.) When you receive an invoice you add it to the file, and then you remove it when you pay. Thus, the A/P is a form of credit that suppliers offer to their purchasers by allowing them to pay for a product or service after it has already been received.
a. Accrual
b. Earnings before interest, taxes, depreciation and amortization
c. Outstanding balance
d. Accounts payable

12. In economics, the concept of the _____ refers to the decision-making time frame of a firm in which at least one factor of production is fixed. Costs which are fixed in the _____ have no impact on a firms decisions. For example a firm can raise output by increasing the amount of labour through overtime.
a. 529 plan
b. 4-4-5 Calendar
c. Long-run
d. Short-run

13. _____ exists when one firm provides goods or services to a customer with an agreement to bill them later, or receive a shipment or service from a supplier under an agreement to pay them later. It can be viewed as an essential element of capitalization in an operating business because it can reduce the required capital investment to operate the business if it is managed properly. _____ is the largest use of capital for a majority of business to business (B2B) sellers in the United States and is a critical source of capital for a majority of all businesses.

   a. Trade credit
   b. 529 plan
   c. Going concern
   d. 4-4-5 Calendar

14. _____ is the provision of resources (such as granting a loan) by one party to another party where that second party does not reimburse the first party immediately, thereby generating a debt, and instead arranges either to repay or return those resources (or material(s) of equal value) at a later date. The first party is called a creditor, also known as a lender, while the second party is called a debtor, also known as a borrower.

Movements of financial capital are normally dependent on either _____ or equity transfers.

   a. Credit
   b. Comparable
   c. Clearing house
   d. Warrant

15. In banking and finance, _____ denotes all activities from the time a commitment is made for a transaction until it is settled. _____ is necessary because the speed of trades is much faster than the cycle time for completing the underlying transaction.

In its widest sense _____ involves the management of post-trading, pre-settlement credit exposures, to ensure that trades are settled in accordance with market rules, even if a buyer or seller should become insolvent prior to settlement.

   a. Clearing house
   b. Share
   c. Procter ' Gamble
   d. Clearing

Chapter 2. Analysis of Solvency, Liquidity, and Financial Flexibility   5

1. The institution most often referenced by the word '_____' is a public or publicly traded _____, the shares of which are traded on a public stock exchange (e.g., the New York Stock Exchange or Nasdaq in the United States) where shares of stock of _____s are bought and sold by and to the general public. Most of the largest businesses in the world are publicly traded _____s. However, the majority of _____s are said to be closely held, privately held or close _____s, meaning that no ready market exists for the trading of shares.

    a. Depository Trust Company
    b. Corporation
    c. Protect
    d. Federal Home Loan Mortgage Corporation

2. The _____ is a financial ratio that measures whether or not a firm has enough resources to pay its debts over the next 12 months. It compares a firm's current assets to its current liabilities. It is expressed as follows:

$$\text{Current ratio} = \frac{\text{Current Assets}}{\text{Current Liabilities}}$$

For example, if WXY Company's current assets are $50,000,000 and its current liabilities are $40,000,000, then its _____ would be $50,000,000 divided by $40,000,000, which equals 1.25.

    a. Debt service coverage ratio
    b. Current ratio
    c. Sustainable growth rate
    d. PEG ratio

3. _____ is a measure of the ability of a debtor to pay their debts as and when they fall due. It is usually expressed as a ratio or a percentage of current liabilities.

For a corporation with a published balance sheet there are various ratios used to calculate a measure of liquidity.

    a. Operating leverage
    b. Invested capital
    c. Operating profit margin
    d. Accounting liquidity

4. In finance, _____ is the ability of an entity to pay its debts with available cash. _____ can also be described as the ability of a corporation to meet its long-term fixed expenses and to accomplish long-term expansion and growth. The better a company's _____, the better it is financially.

    a. Solvency
    b. Capital asset
    c. Political risk
    d. Mid price

5. In finance, the Acid-test or _____ or liquid ratio measures the ability of a company to use its near cash or quick assets to immediately extinguish or retire its current liabilities. Quick assets include those current assets that presumably can be quickly converted to cash at close to their book values.

Generally, the acid test ratio should be 1:1 or better, however this varies widely by industry.

    a. P/E ratio
    b. Net assets
    c. Quick ratio
    d. Financial ratio

Chapter 2. Analysis of Solvency, Liquidity, and Financial Flexibility

6. _____ is a financial metric which represents operating liquidity available to a business. Along with fixed assets such as plant and equipment, _____ is considered a part of operating capital. It is calculated as current assets minus current liabilities.
   a. 4-4-5 Calendar
   b. 529 plan
   c. Working capital management
   d. Working capital

7. In financial accounting, a _____ or statement of cash flows is a financial statement that shows a company's flow of cash. The money coming into the business is called cash inflow, and money going out from the business is called cash outflow. The statement shows how changes in balance sheet and income accounts affect cash and cash equivalents, and breaks the analysis down to operating, investing, and financing activities.
   a. 4-4-5 Calendar
   b. 7-Eleven
   c. Cash flow statement
   d. 529 plan

8. _____ is the balance of the amounts of cash being received and paid by a business during a defined period of time, sometimes tied to a specific project. Measurement of _____ can be used

   - to evaluate the state or performance of a business or project.
   - to determine problems with liquidity. Being profitable does not necessarily mean being liquid. A company can fail because of a shortage of cash, even while profitable.
   - to generate project rate of returns. The time of _____s into and out of projects are used as inputs to financial models such as internal rate of return, and net present value.
   - to examine income or growth of a business when it is believed that accrual accounting concepts do not represent economic realities. Alternately, _____ can be used to 'validate' the net income generated by accrual accounting.

   _____ as a generic term may be used differently depending on context, and certain _____ definitions may be adapted by analysts and users for their own uses. Common terms include operating _____ and free _____.

   _____s can be classified into:

   1. Operational _____s: Cash received or expended as a result of the company's core business activities.
   2. Investment _____s: Cash received or expended through capital expenditure, investments or acquisitions.
   3. Financing _____s: Cash received or expended as a result of financial activities, such as interests and dividends.

   All three together - the net _____ - are necessary to reconcile the beginning cash balance to the ending cash balance. Loan draw downs or equity injections, that is just shifting of capital but no expenditure as such, are not considered in the net _____.

   a. Corporate finance
   b. Real option
   c. Shareholder value
   d. Cash flow

9. _____ or financing is to provide capital (funds), which means money for a project, a person, a business or any other private or public institutions.

Those funds can be allocated for either short term or long term purposes. The health fund is a new way of _____ private healthcare centers.

a. Funding
b. Synthetic CDO
c. Proxy fight
d. Product life cycle

10. _____ is the difference between price and the costs of bringing to market whatever it is that is accounted as an enterprise (whether by harvest, extraction, manufacture, or purchase) in terms of the component costs of delivered goods and/or services and any operating or other expenses.

A key difficulty in measuring profit is in defining costs. Pure economic monetary profits can be zero or negative even in competitive equilibrium when accounted monetized costs exceed monetized price.

a. A Random Walk Down Wall Street
b. Economic profit
c. AAB
d. Accounting profit

11. _____ is a list for goods and materials held available in stock by a business. It is also used for a list of the contents of a household and for a list for testamentary purposes of the possessions of someone who has died. In accounting _____ is considered an asset.

a. AAB
b. ABN Amro
c. A Random Walk Down Wall Street
d. Inventory

12. In accountancy, _____ is a company's average collection period. A low number of days indicates that the company collects its outstanding receivables quickly. Typically, _____ is calculated monthly. The _____ figure is an index of the relationship between outstanding receivables and sales achieved over a given period. The _____ analysis provides general information about the number of days on average that customers take to pay invoices.

a. Net pay
b. Residual value
c. Round-tripping
d. Days sales outstanding

13. _____ is the maximum rate at which a company can grow revenue without having to invest new equity capital. If a company earns a 15% return on equity (ROE), it can grow 15% simply by reinvesting all the earnings in new opportunities and maintaining a stable debt to equity ratio. In order to grow faster, the company would have to invest more equity capital or increase its financial leverage.

a. Sustainable growth rate
b. Price/cash flow ratio
c. Return on capital employed
d. Current ratio

Chapter 3. Valuation

1. In finance, _____ is the process of estimating the potential market value of a financial asset or liability. they can be done on assets (for example, investments in marketable securities such as stocks, options, business enterprises, or intangible assets such as patents and trademarks) or on liabilities (e.g., Bonds issued by a company.) _____s are required in many contexts including investment analysis, capital budgeting, merger and acquisition transactions, financial reporting, taxable events to determine the proper tax liability, and in litigation.
    a. Valuation
    b. Margin
    c. Share
    d. Procter ' Gamble

2. _____ can be regarded as an outcome of mental processes (cognitive process) leading to the selection of a course of action among several alternatives. Every _____ process produces a final choice. The output can be an action or an opinion of choice.
    a. 529 plan
    b. 7-Eleven
    c. 4-4-5 Calendar
    d. Decision making

3. In corporate finance, _____ is an estimate of true economic profit after making corrective adjustments to GAAP accounting, including deducting the opportunity cost of equity capital. GAAP is estimated to ignore US$300 billion in shareholder opportunity costs. _____ can be measured as Net Operating Profit After Taxes(or NOPAT) less the money cost of capital.
    a. Economic value added
    b. ABN Amro
    c. A Random Walk Down Wall Street
    d. AAB

4. _____ or net present worth (NPW) is defined as the total present value (PV) of a time series of cash flows. It is a standard method for using the time value of money to appraise long-term projects. Used for capital budgeting, and widely throughout economics, it measures the excess or shortfall of cash flows, in present value terms, once financing charges are met.
    a. Negative gearing
    b. Net present value
    c. Tax shield
    d. Present value of costs

5. _____ is the value on a given date of a future payment or series of future payments, discounted to reflect the time value of money and other factors such as investment risk. _____ calculations are widely used in business and economics to provide a means to compare cash flows at different times on a meaningful 'like to like' basis.

The most commonly applied model of the time value of money is compound interest.

    a. Negative gearing
    b. Present value
    c. Present value of benefits
    d. Net present value

6. _____ refers to the additional value of a commodity over the cost of commodities used to produce it from the previous stage of production. An example is the price of gasoline at the pump over the price of the oil in it. In national accounts used in macroeconomics, it refers to the contribution of the factors of production, i.e., land, labor, and capital goods, to raising the value of a product and corresponds to the incomes received by the owners of these factors.
    a. Demand shock
    b. Supply shock
    c. Deregulation
    d. Value added

7. _____ is a fee paid on borrowed assets. It is the price paid for the use of borrowed money , or, money earned by deposited funds . Assets that are sometimes lent with _____ include money, shares, consumer goods through hire purchase, major assets such as aircraft, and even entire factories in finance lease arrangements.

Chapter 3. Valuation

a. A Random Walk Down Wall Street
c. AAB
b. Insolvency
d. Interest

8. The institution most often referenced by the word '_____' is a public or publicly traded _____, the shares of which are traded on a public stock exchange (e.g., the New York Stock Exchange or Nasdaq in the United States) where shares of stock of _____s are bought and sold by and to the general public. Most of the largest businesses in the world are publicly traded _____s. However, the majority of _____s are said to be closely held, privately held or close _____s, meaning that no ready market exists for the trading of shares.

a. Protect
c. Federal Home Loan Mortgage Corporation
b. Depository Trust Company
d. Corporation

9. In economics, the concept of the _____ refers to the decision-making time frame of a firm in which at least one factor of production is fixed. Costs which are fixed in the _____ have no impact on a firms decisions. For example a firm can raise output by increasing the amount of labour through overtime.

a. 4-4-5 Calendar
c. 529 plan
b. Long-run
d. Short-run

10. _____ is the concept of adding accumulated interest back to the principal, so that interest is earned on interest from that moment on. The act of declaring interest to be principal is called compounding (i.e., interest is compounded.) A loan, for example, may have its interest compounded every month: in this case, a loan with $100 principal and 1% interest per month would have a balance of $101 at the end of the first month.

a. Compound interest
c. Penny stock
b. 4-4-5 Calendar
d. Risk management

11. An _____ is the price a borrower pays for the use of money they do not own, and the return a lender receives for deferring the use of funds, by lending it to the borrower. _____s are normally expressed as a percentage rate over the period of one year.

_____s targets are also a vital tool of monetary policy and are used to control variables like investment, inflation, and unemployment.

a. AAB
c. Interest rate
b. A Random Walk Down Wall Street
d. ABN Amro

12. The _____, effective annual interest rate, Annual Equivalent Rate (AER) or simply effective rate is the interest rate on a loan or financial product restated from the nominal interest rate as an interest rate with annual compound interest. It is used to compare the annual interest between loans with different compounding terms (daily, monthly, annually, or other.)

The _____ differs in two important respects from the annual percentage rate (APR):

1. the _____ generally does not incorporate one-time charges such as front-end fees;
2. the _____ is (generally) not defined by legal or regulatory authorities (as APR is in many jurisdictions.)

By contrast, the 'effective APR' is used as a legal term, where front-fees and other costs can be included, as defined by local law.

Annual Percentage Yield or effective annual yield is the analogous concept used for savings or investment products, such as a certificate of deposit. .

a. A Random Walk Down Wall Street
b. Effective interest rate
c. ABN Amro
d. AAB

13. _____ is the balance of the amounts of cash being received and paid by a business during a defined period of time, sometimes tied to a specific project. Measurement of _____ can be used

- to evaluate the state or performance of a business or project.
- to determine problems with liquidity. Being profitable does not necessarily mean being liquid. A company can fail because of a shortage of cash, even while profitable.
- to generate project rate of returns. The time of _____s into and out of projects are used as inputs to financial models such as internal rate of return, and net present value.
- to examine income or growth of a business when it is believed that accrual accounting concepts do not represent economic realities. Alternately, _____ can be used to 'validate' the net income generated by accrual accounting.

_____ as a generic term may be used differently depending on context, and certain _____ definitions may be adapted by analysts and users for their own uses. Common terms include operating _____ and free _____.

_____s can be classified into:

1. Operational _____s: Cash received or expended as a result of the company's core business activities.
2. Investment _____s: Cash received or expended through capital expenditure, investments or acquisitions.
3. Financing _____s: Cash received or expended as a result of financial activities, such as interests and dividends.

All three together - the net _____ - are necessary to reconcile the beginning cash balance to the ending cash balance. Loan draw downs or equity injections, that is just shifting of capital but no expenditure as such, are not considered in the net _____.

a. Corporate finance
b. Shareholder value
c. Real option
d. Cash flow

14. _____ are business expenses that are not dependent on the level of production or sales. They tend to be time-related, such as salaries or rents being paid per month. This is in contrast to Variable costs, which are volume-related (and are paid per quantity.)

a. Marginal cost
b. Sliding scale fees
c. Transaction cost
d. Fixed costs

Chapter 3. Valuation

15. _____ are expenses that change in proportion to the activity of a business. In other words, _____ are the sum of marginal costs. It can also be considered normal costs. Along with fixed costs, _____ make up the two components of total cost. Direct Costs, however, are costs that can be associated with a particular cost object.
   a. Fixed costs
   b. Variable costs
   c. Cost accounting
   d. Transaction cost

16. In economics, business, and accounting, a _____ is the value of money that has been used up to produce something, and hence is not available for use anymore. In business, the _____ may be one of acquisition, in which case the amount of money expended to acquire it is counted as _____. In this case, money is the input that is gone in order to acquire the thing.
   a. Fixed costs
   b. Marginal cost
   c. Sliding scale fees
   d. Cost

17. _____ is the difference between price and the costs of bringing to market whatever it is that is accounted as an enterprise (whether by harvest, extraction, manufacture, or purchase) in terms of the component costs of delivered goods and/or services and any operating or other expenses.

A key difficulty in measuring profit is in defining costs. Pure economic monetary profits can be zero or negative even in competitive equilibrium when accounted monetized costs exceed monetized price.

   a. AAB
   b. Economic profit
   c. A Random Walk Down Wall Street
   d. Accounting profit

18. The _____ is an expected return that the provider of capital plans to earn on their investment.

Capital (money) used for funding a business should earn returns for the capital providers who risk their capital. For an investment to be worthwhile, the expected return on capital must be greater than the _____.

   a. Capital intensity
   b. Weighted average cost of capital
   c. 4-4-5 Calendar
   d. Cost of capital

19. A '_____' is a 'Charge' that is paid to obtain the right to delay a payment. Essentially, the payer purchases the right to make a given payment in the future instead of in the Present. The '_____', or 'Charge' that must be paid to delay the payment, is simply the difference between what the payment amount would be if it were paid in the present and what the payment amount would be paid if it were paid in the future.
   a. Discount
   b. Value at risk
   c. Risk aversion
   d. Risk modeling

20. The _____ is an interest rate a central bank charges depository institutions that borrow reserves from it.

The term _____ has two meanings:

- the same as interest rate; the term 'discount' does not refer to the meaning of the word, but to the purpose of using the quantity, such as computations of present value, e.g. net present value / discounted cash flow

- the annual effective _____, which is the annual interest divided by the capital including that interest; this rate is lower than the interest rate; it corresponds to using the value after a year as the nominal value, and seeing the initial value as the nominal value minus a discount; it is used for Treasury Bills and similar financial instruments

The annual effective _____ is the annual interest divided by the capital including that interest, which is the interest rate divided by 100% plus the interest rate. It is the annual discount factor to be applied to the future cash flow, to find the discount, subtracted from a future value to find the value one year earlier.

For example, suppose there is a government bond that sells for $95 and pays $100 in a year's time.

a. Discount rate
b. Black-Scholes
c. Fisher equation
d. Stochastic volatility

21. _____ means regulating, adapting or settling in a variety of contexts:

In commercial law, _____ means the settlement of a loss incurred on insured goods. The calculation of the amounts of compensation to be paid by or to the several interests is a complicated matter. It involves much detail and arithmetic, and requires a full and accurate knowledge of the principles of the subject.

a. Equity method
b. Intelligent investor
c. Asset recovery
d. Adjustment

Chapter 3. Valuation

22. The term _____ has three unrelated technical definitions, and is also used in a variety of non-technical ways.

- In financial economics, it refers to any asset used to make money, as opposed to assets used for personal enjoyment or consumption. This is an important distinction because two people can disagree sharply about the value of personal assets, one person might think a sports car is more valuable than a pickup truck, another person might have the opposite taste. But if an asset is held for the purpose of making money, taste has nothing to do with it, only differences of opinion about how much money the asset will produce. With the further assumption that people agree on the probability distribution of future cash flows, it is possible to have an objective _____ pricing model. Even without the assumption of agreement, it is possible to set rational limits on _____ value.
- In governmental accounting, it is defined as any asset used in operations with an initial useful life extending beyond one reporting period. Generally, government managers have a 'stewardship' duty to maintain _____s under their control. See International Public Sector Accounting Standards for details.
- In US tax accounting, it is defined as any property other than a list of exceptions. The main exceptions are anything held for sale, and any real estate or depreciable property used in business. Almost everything you own and use for personal purposes, pleasure or investment is a _____. If something is a _____ for tax purposes, gains or losses on sale or disposition are capital gains or capital losses. For individuals, however, capital losses on property held for personal use are generally not deductible. See the IRS publication Tax Facts about Capital Gains and Losses for details.

A well-known financial accounting textbook advises that the term be avoided except in tax accounting because it is used in so many different senses, not all of them well-defined. For example it is often used as a synonym for fixed assets or for investments in securities.

A common non-technical usage occurs when people ask that employees or the environment or something else be treated as a _____.

a. Capital asset
b. Settlement date
c. Solvency
d. Political risk

23. In finance, the _____ is used to determine a theoretically appropriate required rate of return of an asset, if that asset is to be added to an already well-diversified portfolio, given that asset's non-diversifiable risk. The model takes into account the asset's sensitivity to non-diversifiable risk (also known as systemic risk or market risk), often represented by the quantity beta (β) in the financial industry, as well as the expected return of the market and the expected return of a theoretical risk-free asset.

The model was introduced by Jack Treynor (1961, 1962), William Sharpe (1964), John Lintner (1965a,b) and Jan Mossin (1966) independently, building on the earlier work of Harry Markowitz on diversification and modern portfolio theory.

a. Cox-Ingersoll-Ross model
b. Random walk hypothesis
c. Hull-White model
d. Capital asset pricing model

24. In business and accounting, _____s are everything of value that is owned by a person or company. The balance sheet of a firm records the monetary value of the _____s owned by the firm. The two major _____ classes are tangible _____s and intangible _____s.

a. EBITDA
b. Asset
c. Accounts payable
d. Income

25. _____ is a list for goods and materials held available in stock by a business. It is also used for a list of the contents of a household and for a list for testamentary purposes of the possessions of someone who has died. In accounting _____ is considered an asset.

a. AAB
b. A Random Walk Down Wall Street
c. ABN Amro
d. Inventory

Chapter 4. Inventory Management

1. The institution most often referenced by the word '_____' is a public or publicly traded _____, the shares of which are traded on a public stock exchange (e.g., the New York Stock Exchange or Nasdaq in the United States) where shares of stock of _____s are bought and sold by and to the general public. Most of the largest businesses in the world are publicly traded _____s. However, the majority of _____s are said to be closely held, privately held or close _____s, meaning that no ready market exists for the trading of shares.
   - a. Protect
   - b. Corporation
   - c. Federal Home Loan Mortgage Corporation
   - d. Depository Trust Company

2. A _____ is the system of organizations, people, technology, activities, information and resources involved in moving a product or service from supplier to customer. _____ activities transform natural resources, raw materials and components into a finished product that is delivered to the end customer. In sophisticated _____ systems, used products may re-enter the _____ at any point where residual value is recyclable.
   - a. 7-Eleven
   - b. Supply chain
   - c. 4-4-5 Calendar
   - d. 529 plan

3. _____, in bookkeeping, refers to assets, liabilities, income, and expenses recorded on individual pages of the so called book of final entry or ledger. Changes in _____ value are made by chronologically posting debit (DR) and credit (CR) entries to its page. Examples of _____s are cash, _____s receivable, mortgages, loans, land and buildings, common stock, sales, services provided, wages, and payroll overhead.
   - a. Option
   - b. Alpha
   - c. Accretion
   - d. Account

4. _____ is a file or account that contains money that a person or company owes to suppliers, but hasn't paid yet (a form of debt.) When you receive an invoice you add it to the file, and then you remove it when you pay. Thus, the A/P is a form of credit that suppliers offer to their purchasers by allowing them to pay for a product or service after it has already been received.
   - a. Accrual
   - b. Outstanding balance
   - c. Earnings before interest, taxes, depreciation and amortization
   - d. Accounts payable

5. _____s are goods that have completed the manufacturing process but have not yet been sold or distributed to the end user.

Manufacturing has three classes of inventory:

1. Raw material
2. Work in process
3. _____s

A good purchased as a 'raw material' goes into the manufacture of a product. A good only partially completed during the manufacturing process is called 'work in process'. When the good is completed as to manufacturing but not yet sold or distributed to the end-user is called a '_____'.

   - a. 7-Eleven
   - b. 4-4-5 Calendar
   - c. 529 plan
   - d. Finished good

Chapter 4. Inventory Management

6. _____ is a list for goods and materials held available in stock by a business. It is also used for a list of the contents of a household and for a list for testamentary purposes of the possessions of someone who has died. In accounting _____ is considered an asset.
   a. Inventory
   b. A Random Walk Down Wall Street
   c. ABN Amro
   d. AAB

7. In economics, business, and accounting, a _____ is the value of money that has been used up to produce something, and hence is not available for use anymore. In business, the _____ may be one of acquisition, in which case the amount of money expended to acquire it is counted as _____. In this case, money is the input that is gone in order to acquire the thing.
   a. Fixed costs
   b. Sliding scale fees
   c. Marginal cost
   d. Cost

8. The _____ is an expected return that the provider of capital plans to earn on their investment.

Capital (money) used for funding a business should earn returns for the capital providers who risk their capital. For an investment to be worthwhile, the expected return on capital must be greater than the _____.

   a. Capital intensity
   b. Weighted average cost of capital
   c. 4-4-5 Calendar
   d. Cost of capital

9. _____ is the level of inventory that minimizes the total inventory holding costs and ordering costs. The framework used to determine this order quantity is also known as Wilson _____ Model. The model was developed by F. W. Harris in 1913.
   a. ABN Amro
   b. AAB
   c. Economic order quantity
   d. A Random Walk Down Wall Street

10. The _____ is the level of inventory when a fresh order should be made with suppliers to bring the inventory up by the Economic order quantity ('EOQ'.)

The _____ for replenishment of stock occurs when the level of inventory drops down to zero. In view of instantaneous replenishment of stock the level of inventory jumps to the original level from zero level.

   a. 7-Eleven
   b. 529 plan
   c. Reorder point
   d. 4-4-5 Calendar

11. _____ is a term used by inventory specialists to describe a level of extra stock that is maintained below the cycle stock to buffer against stockouts. _____ exists to counter uncertainties in supply and demand. _____ is defined as extra units of inventory carried as protection against possible stockouts .(shortfall in raw material or packaging.)
   a. Funding
   b. Counting house
   c. Golden parachute
   d. Safety stock

12. A '_____' is a 'Charge' that is paid to obtain the right to delay a payment. Essentially, the payer purchases the right to make a given payment in the future instead of in the Present. The '_____', or 'Charge' that must be paid to delay the payment, is simply the difference between what the payment amount would be if it were paid in the present and what the payment amount would be paid if it were paid in the future.

Chapter 4. Inventory Management

a. Discount
c. Risk aversion
b. Value at risk
d. Risk modeling

13. In business and finance, a _____ (also referred to as equity _____) of stock means a _____ of ownership in a corporation (company.) In the plural, stocks is often used as a synonym for _____s especially in the United States, but it is less commonly used that way outside of North America.

In the United Kingdom, South Africa, and Australia, stock can also refer to completely different financial instruments such as government bonds or, less commonly, to all kinds of marketable securities.

a. Procter ' Gamble
c. Margin
b. Bucket shop
d. Share

14. _____ is the balance of the amounts of cash being received and paid by a business during a defined period of time, sometimes tied to a specific project. Measurement of _____ can be used

- to evaluate the state or performance of a business or project.
- to determine problems with liquidity. Being profitable does not necessarily mean being liquid. A company can fail because of a shortage of cash, even while profitable.
- to generate project rate of returns. The time of _____s into and out of projects are used as inputs to financial models such as internal rate of return, and net present value.
- to examine income or growth of a business when it is believed that accrual accounting concepts do not represent economic realities. Alternately, _____ can be used to 'validate' the net income generated by accrual accounting.

_____ as a generic term may be used differently depending on context, and certain _____ definitions may be adapted by analysts and users for their own uses. Common terms include operating _____ and free _____.

_____s can be classified into:

1. Operational _____s: Cash received or expended as a result of the company's core business activities.
2. Investment _____s: Cash received or expended through capital expenditure, investments or acquisitions.
3. Financing _____s: Cash received or expended as a result of financial activities, such as interests and dividends.

All three together - the net _____ - are necessary to reconcile the beginning cash balance to the ending cash balance. Loan draw downs or equity injections, that is just shifting of capital but no expenditure as such, are not considered in the net _____.

a. Real option
c. Shareholder value
b. Corporate finance
d. Cash flow

15. _____ are horizontal lines drawn on an statistical process control chart, usually at a distance of >±3 standard deviations of the plotted statistic from the statistic's mean.

Chapter 4. Inventory Management

For normally distributed statistics, the area bracketed by the _____ will on average contain 99.73% of all the plot points on the chart, as long as the process is and remains in statistical control.

_____ should not be confused with tolerance limits, which are completely independent of the distribution of the plotted sample statistic.

a. Control limits
b. 529 plan
c. 7-Eleven
d. 4-4-5 Calendar

16. The _____ is an equation that equals the cost of goods sold divided by the average inventory. Average inventory equals beginning inventory plus ending inventory divided by 2.

The formula for _____:

$$\text{Inventory Turnover} = \frac{\text{Cost of Goods Sold}}{\text{Average Inventory}}$$

The formula for average inventory:

$$\text{Average Inventory} = \frac{\text{Beginning inventory} + \text{Ending inventory}}{2}$$

A low turnover rate may point to overstocking, obsolescence, or deficiencies in the product line or marketing effort.

a. Information ratio
b. Inventory turnover
c. Operating leverage
d. Earnings yield

17. _____ is an inventory strategy implemented to improve the return on investment of a business by reducing in-process inventory and its associated carrying costs. In order to achieve _____ the process must have signals of what is going on elsewhere within the process. This means that the process is often driven by a series of signals, which can be Kanban, that tell production processes when to make the next part.

a. Greed and fear
b. Pac-Man defense
c. Just-in-time
d. Debtor-in-possession financing

18. In finance, a _____ is a position established in one market in an attempt to offset exposure to the price risk of an equal but opposite obligation or position in another market -- usually, but not always, in the context of one's commercial activity. Hedging is a strategy designed to minimize exposure to such business risks as a sharp contraction in demand for one's inventory, while still allowing the business to profit from producing and maintaining that inventory. A typical hedger might be a farmer with 2000 acres of unharvested wheat in the ground, who would rather tend his crop without the distraction of uncertain prices.

a. 529 plan
b. 4-4-5 Calendar
c. 7-Eleven
d. Hedge

Chapter 4. Inventory Management

19. Procter is a surname, and may also refer to:

    - Bryan Waller Procter (pseud. Barry Cornwall), English poet
    - Goodwin Procter, American law firm
    - _____, consumer products multinational

a. Procter ' Gamble
c. Valuation
b. Clearing house
d. Bucket shop

20. _____ is defined by APICS as a method for the effective planning of all resources of a manufacturing company. Ideally, it addresses operational planning in units, financial planning in dollars, and has a simulation capability to answer 'what-if' questions and extension of closed-loop _____. Manufacturing Resource Planning - Around 1980, over-frequent changes in sales forecasts, entailing continual readjustments in production, as well as the unsuitability of the parameters fixed by the system, led _____ to evolve into a new concept : _____.

This is not exclusively a software function, but a marriage of people skills, dedication to data base accuracy, and computer resources.

a. 7-Eleven
c. 4-4-5 Calendar
b. 529 plan
d. Manufacturing resource planning

Chapter 5. Accounts Receivable Management

1. _____ is the discipline of identifying, monitoring and limiting risks. In some cases the acceptable risk may be near zero. Risks can come from accidents, natural causes and disasters as well as deliberate attacks from an adversary.
   a. Risk Management
   b. 4-4-5 Calendar
   c. FIFO
   d. Penny stock

2. _____ is a business buzz term, which implies that the ultimate measure of a company's success is to enrich shareholders. It became popular during the 1980s, and is particularly associated with former CEO of General Electric, Jack Welch. In March 2009, Welch openly turned his back on the concept, calling _____ 'the dumbest idea in the world'.

For a publicly traded company, _____ is the part of its capitalization that is equity as opposed to long-term debt. In the case of only one type of stock, this would roughly be the number of outstanding shares times current shareprice. Things like dividends augment _____ while issuing of shares (stock options) lower it. This _____ added should be compared to average/required increase in value, aka cost of capital.

For a privately held company, the value of the firm after debt must be estimated using one of several valuation methods, s.a. discounted cash flow or others.

   a. Cash flow
   b. Restricted stock
   c. Commercial paper
   d. Shareholder value

3. _____ exists when one firm provides goods or services to a customer with an agreement to bill them later, or receive a shipment or service from a supplier under an agreement to pay them later. It can be viewed as an essential element of capitalization in an operating business because it can reduce the required capital investment to operate the business if it is managed properly. _____ is the largest use of capital for a majority of business to business (B2B) sellers in the United States and is a critical source of capital for a majority of all businesses.
   a. 529 plan
   b. Going concern
   c. 4-4-5 Calendar
   d. Trade credit

4. _____ is the provision of resources (such as granting a loan) by one party to another party where that second party does not reimburse the first party immediately, thereby generating a debt, and instead arranges either to repay or return those resources (or material(s) of equal value) at a later date. The first party is called a creditor, also known as a lender, while the second party is called a debtor, also known as a borrower.

Movements of financial capital are normally dependent on either _____ or equity transfers.

   a. Clearing house
   b. Warrant
   c. Comparable
   d. Credit

5. _____ is a financial metric which represents operating liquidity available to a business. Along with fixed assets such as plant and equipment, _____ is considered a part of operating capital. It is calculated as current assets minus current liabilities.
   a. 4-4-5 Calendar
   b. 529 plan
   c. Working capital management
   d. Working capital

Chapter 5. Accounts Receivable Management

6. _____, consists of the buying and selling of products or services over electronic systems such as the Internet and other computer networks. The amount of trade conducted electronically has grown extraordinarily with widespread Internet usage. The use of commerce is conducted in this way, spurring and drawing on innovations in electronic funds transfer, supply chain management, Internet marketing, online transaction processing, electronic data interchange (EDI), inventory management systems, and automated data collection systems.
   - a. AAB
   - b. ABN Amro
   - c. A Random Walk Down Wall Street
   - d. Electronic commerce

7. _____ is a list for goods and materials held available in stock by a business. It is also used for a list of the contents of a household and for a list for testamentary purposes of the possessions of someone who has died. In accounting _____ is considered an asset.
   - a. AAB
   - b. A Random Walk Down Wall Street
   - c. ABN Amro
   - d. Inventory

8. A _____ is a letter sent by a customer to a supplier, to inform that supplier that their invoice has been paid. If the customer is paying by cheque, the _____ often accompanies the cheque.

   _____s are not mandatory, however they are seen as a courtesy because they help the supplier's accounts department to match invoices with payments.

   - a. Construction in Progress
   - b. Remittance advice
   - c. Fixed asset
   - d. Petty cash

9. A _____ is the maximum amount of credit that a financial institution or other lender will extend to a debtor for a particular line of credit. For example, the maximum that a credit card company will allow a card holder to borrow at any given point on a specific card.

   This limit is based on a variety of factors ranging from an individual's ability to make interest payments, an organization's cashflow and/or ability to repay the principal, to the credit standards employed by the lender.

   - a. 4-4-5 Calendar
   - b. 529 plan
   - c. 7-Eleven
   - d. Credit limit

10. The institution most often referenced by the word '_____' is a public or publicly traded _____, the shares of which are traded on a public stock exchange (e.g., the New York Stock Exchange or Nasdaq in the United States) where shares of stock of _____s are bought and sold by and to the general public. Most of the largest businesses in the world are publicly traded _____s. However, the majority of _____s are said to be closely held, privately held or close _____s, meaning that no ready market exists for the trading of shares.
    - a. Federal Home Loan Mortgage Corporation
    - b. Depository Trust Company
    - c. Protect
    - d. Corporation

11. In lending agreements, _____ is a borrower's pledge of specific property to a lender, to secure repayment of a loan. The _____ serves as protection for a lender against a borrower's risk of default - that is, a borrower failing to pay the principal and interest under the terms of a loan obligation. If a borrower does default on a loan (due to insolvency or other event), that borrower forfeits (gives up) the property pledged as _____ *ollateral* - and the lender then becomes the owner of the _____.

a. Nominal value
c. Refinancing risk
b. Future-oriented
d. Collateral

12. A _____ is a business that pursues payments on debts owed by individuals or businesses. Most collection agencies operate as agents of creditors and collect debts for a fee or percentage of the total amount owed. Some agencies, sometimes referred to as 'debt buyers', purchase debts from creditors for a fraction of the value of the debt and pursue the debtor for the full balance.
   a. Guaranteed consumer funding
   b. Commercial hard money
   c. Partial Payment
   d. Collection agency

13. _____ is the method by which one calculates the creditworthiness of a business or organization. The audited financial statements of a large company might be analyzed when it issues or has issued bonds. Or, a bank may analyze the financial statements of a small business before making or renewing a commercial loan.
   a. Capital note
   b. Credit crunch
   c. Credit analysis
   d. Credit report monitoring

14. A '_____' is a 'Charge' that is paid to obtain the right to delay a payment. Essentially, the payer purchases the right to make a given payment in the future instead of in the Present. The '_____', or 'Charge' that must be paid to delay the payment, is simply the difference between what the payment amount would be if it were paid in the present and what the payment amount would be paid if it were paid in the future.
   a. Risk aversion
   b. Risk modeling
   c. Value at risk
   d. Discount

15. In banking and finance, _____ denotes all activities from the time a commitment is made for a transaction until it is settled. _____ is necessary because the speed of trades is much faster than the cycle time for completing the underlying transaction.

In its widest sense _____ involves the management of post-trading, pre-settlement credit exposures, to ensure that trades are settled in accordance with market rules, even if a buyer or seller should become insolvent prior to settlement.

   a. Procter ' Gamble
   b. Clearing
   c. Clearing house
   d. Share

Chapter 6. Credit Policy and Collections

1. The institution most often referenced by the word '_____' is a public or publicly traded _____, the shares of which are traded on a public stock exchange (e.g., the New York Stock Exchange or Nasdaq in the United States) where shares of stock of _____s are bought and sold by and to the general public. Most of the largest businesses in the world are publicly traded _____s. However, the majority of _____s are said to be closely held, privately held or close _____s, meaning that no ready market exists for the trading of shares.

   a. Federal Home Loan Mortgage Corporation
   b. Protect
   c. Depository Trust Company
   d. Corporation

2. _____ is the balance of the amounts of cash being received and paid by a business during a defined period of time, sometimes tied to a specific project. Measurement of _____ can be used

   - to evaluate the state or performance of a business or project.
   - to determine problems with liquidity. Being profitable does not necessarily mean being liquid. A company can fail because of a shortage of cash, even while profitable.
   - to generate project rate of returns. The time of _____s into and out of projects are used as inputs to financial models such as internal rate of return, and net present value.
   - to examine income or growth of a business when it is believed that accrual accounting concepts do not represent economic realities. Alternately, _____ can be used to 'validate' the net income generated by accrual accounting.

   _____ as a generic term may be used differently depending on context, and certain _____ definitions may be adapted by analysts and users for their own uses. Common terms include operating _____ and free _____.

   _____s can be classified into:

   1. Operational _____s: Cash received or expended as a result of the company's core business activities.
   2. Investment _____s: Cash received or expended through capital expenditure, investments or acquisitions.
   3. Financing _____s: Cash received or expended as a result of financial activities, such as interests and dividends.

   All three together - the net _____ - are necessary to reconcile the beginning cash balance to the ending cash balance. Loan draw downs or equity injections, that is just shifting of capital but no expenditure as such, are not considered in the net _____.

   a. Corporate finance
   b. Real option
   c. Cash flow
   d. Shareholder value

3. _____ is the provision of resources (such as granting a loan) by one party to another party where that second party does not reimburse the first party immediately, thereby generating a debt, and instead arranges either to repay or return those resources (or material(s) of equal value) at a later date. The first party is called a creditor, also known as a lender, while the second party is called a debtor, also known as a borrower.

   Movements of financial capital are normally dependent on either _____ or equity transfers.

a. Clearing house
c. Credit
b. Warrant
d. Comparable

4. _____ or net present worth (NPW) is defined as the total present value (PV) of a time series of cash flows. It is a standard method for using the time value of money to appraise long-term projects. Used for capital budgeting, and widely throughout economics, it measures the excess or shortfall of cash flows, in present value terms, once financing charges are met.
   a. Present value of costs
   b. Tax shield
   c. Negative gearing
   d. Net present value

5. _____ is the difference between price and the costs of bringing to market whatever it is that is accounted as an enterprise (whether by harvest, extraction, manufacture, or purchase) in terms of the component costs of delivered goods and/or services and any operating or other expenses.

A key difficulty in measuring profit is in defining costs. Pure economic monetary profits can be zero or negative even in competitive equilibrium when accounted monetized costs exceed monetized price.

   a. Accounting profit
   b. AAB
   c. A Random Walk Down Wall Street
   d. Economic profit

6. _____ is the value on a given date of a future payment or series of future payments, discounted to reflect the time value of money and other factors such as investment risk. _____ calculations are widely used in business and economics to provide a means to compare cash flows at different times on a meaningful 'like to like' basis.

The most commonly applied model of the time value of money is compound interest.

   a. Negative gearing
   b. Present value of benefits
   c. Present value
   d. Net present value

7. _____ is a banking term for Originating depository financial institution, used in connection with Automated Clearing Houses (ACH.) In the ACH flow, the _____ acts as the interface between the Federal Reserve or ACH network and the originator of the transaction. The _____ warrants to the ACH network that the transactions it transmits to the network comply with the rules.
   a. A Random Walk Down Wall Street
   b. ODFI
   c. ABN Amro
   d. AAB

8. A '_____' is a 'Charge' that is paid to obtain the right to delay a payment. Essentially, the payer purchases the right to make a given payment in the future instead of in the Present. The '_____', or 'Charge' that must be paid to delay the payment, is simply the difference between what the payment amount would be if it were paid in the present and what the payment amount would be paid if it were paid in the future.
   a. Value at risk
   b. Risk modeling
   c. Risk aversion
   d. Discount

Chapter 6. Credit Policy and Collections

9. _____, in bookkeeping, refers to assets, liabilities, income, and expenses recorded on individual pages of the so called book of final entry or ledger. Changes in _____ value are made by chronologically posting debit (DR) and credit (CR) entries to its page. Examples of _____s are cash, _____s receivable, mortgages, loans, land and buildings, common stock, sales, services provided, wages, and payroll overhead.
   a. Option
   b. Alpha
   c. Accretion
   d. Account

10. _____ is a file or account that contains money that a person or company owes to suppliers, but hasn't paid yet (a form of debt.) When you receive an invoice you add it to the file, and then you remove it when you pay. Thus, the A/P is a form of credit that suppliers offer to their purchasers by allowing them to pay for a product or service after it has already been received.
   a. Earnings before interest, taxes, depreciation and amortization
   b. Outstanding balance
   c. Accrual
   d. Accounts payable

11. A _____ is a business that pursues payments on debts owed by individuals or businesses. Most collection agencies operate as agents of creditors and collect debts for a fee or percentage of the total amount owed. Some agencies, sometimes referred to as 'debt buyers', purchase debts from creditors for a fraction of the value of the debt and pursue the debtor for the full balance.
   a. Commercial hard money
   b. Partial Payment
   c. Guaranteed consumer funding
   d. Collection agency

12. In accountancy, _____ is a company's average collection period. A low number of days indicates that the company collects its outstanding receivables quickly. Typically, _____ is calculated monthly. The _____ figure is an index of the relationship between outstanding receivables and sales achieved over a given period. The _____ analysis provides general information about the number of days on average that customers take to pay invoices.
   a. Round-tripping
   b. Net pay
   c. Residual value
   d. Days sales outstanding

13. _____ is one of a series of accounting transactions dealing with the billing of customers who owe money to a person, company or organization for goods and services that have been provided to the customer. In most business entities this is typically done by generating an invoice and mailing or electronically delivering it to the customer, who in turn must pay it within an established timeframe called credit or payment terms.

An example of a common payment term is Net 30, meaning payment is due in the amount of the invoice 30 days from the date of invoice.

   a. Income
   b. Impaired asset
   c. Accounting methods
   d. Accounts receivable

14. _____ is one of the accounting liquidity ratios, a financial ratio. This ratio measures the number of times, on average, receivables (e.g. Accounts Receivable) are collected during the period. A popular variant of the _____ is to convert it into an Average Collection Period in terms of days.
   a. Receivables turnover ratio
   b. Return on equity
   c. PEG ratio
   d. Sharpe ratio

Chapter 6. Credit Policy and Collections

15. A _____ is a fungible, negotiable instrument representing financial value. They are broadly categorized into debt securities (such as banknotes, bonds and debentures), and equity securities; e.g., common stocks. The company or other entity issuing the _____ is called the issuer.
   a. Tracking stock
   b. Securities lending
   c. Book entry
   d. Security

16. _____ is a list for goods and materials held available in stock by a business. It is also used for a list of the contents of a household and for a list for testamentary purposes of the possessions of someone who has died. In accounting _____ is considered an asset.
   a. A Random Walk Down Wall Street
   b. ABN Amro
   c. AAB
   d. Inventory

17. _____ (or spoilage) refers to the process by which tissues of dead organisms break down into simpler forms of matter. Such a breakdown of dead organisms is essential for new growth and development of living organisms because it recycles the finite chemical constituents and frees up the limited physical space in the biome. Bodies of living organisms begin to decompose shortly after death.
   a. 4-4-5 Calendar
   b. 7-Eleven
   c. 529 plan
   d. Decomposition

18. In probability theory and statistics, the _____ of a random variable, probability distribution averaging the squared distance of its possible values from the expected value (mean.) Whereas the mean is a way to describe the location of a distribution, the _____ is a way to capture its scale or degree of being spread out. The unit of _____ is the square of the unit of the original variable.
   a. Semivariance
   b. Variance
   c. Harmonic mean
   d. Monte Carlo methods

19. In statistics, _____ refers to techniques for the modeling and analysis of numerical data consisting of values of a dependent variable and of one or more independent variables The dependent variable in the regression equation is modeled as a function of the independent variables, corresponding parameters, and an error term. The error term is treated as a random variable.
   a. 7-Eleven
   b. 4-4-5 Calendar
   c. Regression analysis
   d. 529 plan

Chapter 7. Managing Payables and Accruals

1. _____, in bookkeeping, refers to assets, liabilities, income, and expenses recorded on individual pages of the so called book of final entry or ledger. Changes in _____ value are made by chronologically posting debit (DR) and credit (CR) entries to its page. Examples of _____s are cash, _____s receivable, mortgages, loans, land and buildings, common stock, sales, services provided, wages, and payroll overhead.
   a. Alpha
   b. Account
   c. Accretion
   d. Option

2. _____ is a file or account that contains money that a person or company owes to suppliers, but hasn't paid yet (a form of debt.) When you receive an invoice you add it to the file, and then you remove it when you pay. Thus, the A/P is a form of credit that suppliers offer to their purchasers by allowing them to pay for a product or service after it has already been received.
   a. Outstanding balance
   b. Accrual
   c. Earnings before interest, taxes, depreciation and amortization
   d. Accounts payable

3. A '_____' is a 'Charge' that is paid to obtain the right to delay a payment. Essentially, the payer purchases the right to make a given payment in the future instead of in the Present. The '_____', or 'Charge' that must be paid to delay the payment, is simply the difference between what the payment amount would be if it were paid in the present and what the payment amount would be paid if it were paid in the future.
   a. Risk aversion
   b. Risk modeling
   c. Value at risk
   d. Discount

4. In economics, the concept of the _____ refers to the decision-making time frame of a firm in which at least one factor of production is fixed. Costs which are fixed in the _____ have no impact on a firms decisions. For example a firm can raise output by increasing the amount of labour through overtime.
   a. 4-4-5 Calendar
   b. 529 plan
   c. Long-run
   d. Short-run

5. _____ is the balance of the amounts of cash being received and paid by a business during a defined period of time, sometimes tied to a specific project. Measurement of _____ can be used

   - to evaluate the state or performance of a business or project.
   - to determine problems with liquidity. Being profitable does not necessarily mean being liquid. A company can fail because of a shortage of cash, even while profitable.
   - to generate project rate of returns. The time of _____s into and out of projects are used as inputs to financial models such as internal rate of return, and net present value.
   - to examine income or growth of a business when it is believed that accrual accounting concepts do not represent economic realities. Alternately, _____ can be used to 'validate' the net income generated by accrual accounting.

   _____ as a generic term may be used differently depending on context, and certain _____ definitions may be adapted by analysts and users for their own uses. Common terms include operating _____ and free _____.

Chapter 7. Managing Payables and Accruals

_____s can be classified into:

1. Operational _____s: Cash received or expended as a result of the company's core business activities.
2. Investment _____s: Cash received or expended through capital expenditure, investments or acquisitions.
3. Financing _____s: Cash received or expended as a result of financial activities, such as interests and dividends.

All three together - the net _____ - are necessary to reconcile the beginning cash balance to the ending cash balance. Loan draw downs or equity injections, that is just shifting of capital but no expenditure as such, are not considered in the net _____.

a. Real option
b. Cash flow
c. Corporate finance
d. Shareholder value

6. _____ is the act of consigning, which is placing a person or thing in the hand of another, but retaining ownership until the goods are sold or person is transferred. This may be done for shipping, transfer of prisoners, or for sale in a store (i.e. a _____ shop.)

Features of _____ are as follows: 1)The Relation between the two parties is that of consignor and consignee and not that of buyer and seller 2)The consignor is entitled to receive all the expenses in connection with _____ 3)The consignee is not responsible for damage of goods during transport or any other procedure.

a. 4-4-5 Calendar
b. 7-Eleven
c. 529 plan
d. Consignment

7. The free _____ of a public company is an estimate of the proportion of shares that are not held by large owners and that are not stock with sales restrictions (restricted stock that cannot be sold until they become unrestricted stock.)

The free _____ or a public _____ is usually defined as being all shares held by investors other than:

- shares held by owners owning more than 5% of all shares (those could be institutional investors, 'strategic shareholders,' founders, executives, and other insiders' holdings)
- restricted stocks (granted to executives that can be, but don't have to be, registered insiders)
- insider holdings (it is assumed that insiders hold stock for the very long term)

The free _____ is an important criterion in quoting a share on the stock market.

Chapter 7. Managing Payables and Accruals

To _____ a company means to list its shares on a public stock exchange through an initial public offering (or 'flotation'.)

- Open market
- Outstanding shares
- Market capitalization
- Public _____ *loat*
- Reverse takeover

a. Trade finance
c. Synthetic CDO
b. Golden parachute
d. Float

8. A _____ is an association of two or more individuals, companies, organizations or governments (or any combination of these entities) with the objective of participating in a common activity or pooling their resources for achieving a common goal.
a. 4-4-5 Calendar
c. 7-Eleven
b. 529 plan
d. Consortium

9. _____ refer to services provided by the finance industry.

The finance industry encompasses a broad range of organizations that deal with the management of money. Among these organizations are banks, credit card companies, insurance companies, consumer finance companies, stock brokerages, investment funds and some government sponsored enterprises.

a. Financial Services
c. Delta hedging
b. Cost of carry
d. Financial instruments

10. The institution most often referenced by the word '_____' is a public or publicly traded _____, the shares of which are traded on a public stock exchange (e.g., the New York Stock Exchange or Nasdaq in the United States) where shares of stock of _____s are bought and sold by and to the general public. Most of the largest businesses in the world are publicly traded _____s. However, the majority of _____s are said to be closely held, privately held or close _____s, meaning that no ready market exists for the trading of shares.
a. Federal Home Loan Mortgage Corporation
c. Depository Trust Company
b. Protect
d. Corporation

11. _____ refers to a business or organization attempting to acquire goods or services to accomplish the goals of the enterprise. Though there are several organizations that attempt to set standards in the _____ process, processes can vary greatly between organizations. Typically the word '_____' is not used interchangeably with the word 'procurement', since procurement typically includes Expediting, Supplier Quality, and Traffic and Logistics (T'L) in addition to _____.
a. 7-Eleven
c. 4-4-5 Calendar
b. 529 plan
d. Purchasing

Chapter 7. Managing Payables and Accruals

12. Accrual, in accounting, describes the accounting method known as _____, whereby revenues and expenses are recognized when they are accrued, i.e. accumulated (earned or incurred), regardless when the actual cash is received or paid out.

E.g. a company delivers a product to a customer who will pay for it 30 days later in the next fiscal year starting a week after the delivery. The company recognizes the proceeds as a revenue in its current income statement still for the fiscal year of the delivery, even though it will get paid in cash during the following accounting period.

a. AAB
b. Accrual basis
c. ABN Amro
d. A Random Walk Down Wall Street

Chapter 8. The Payment System and Financial Institution Relationships

1. The free _____ of a public company is an estimate of the proportion of shares that are not held by large owners and that are not stock with sales restrictions (restricted stock that cannot be sold until they become unrestricted stock.)

The free _____ or a public _____ is usually defined as being all shares held by investors other than:

- shares held by owners owning more than 5% of all shares (those could be institutional investors, 'strategic shareholders,' founders, executives, and other insiders' holdings)
- restricted stocks (granted to executives that can be, but don't have to be, registered insiders)
- insider holdings (it is assumed that insiders hold stock for the very long term)

The free _____ is an important criterion in quoting a share on the stock market.

To _____ a company means to list its shares on a public stock exchange through an initial public offering (or 'flotation'.)

- Open market
- Outstanding shares
- Market capitalization
- Public _____ *loat*
- Reverse takeover

a. Trade finance
b. Float
c. Synthetic CDO
d. Golden parachute

2. _____ or net present worth (NPW) is defined as the total present value (PV) of a time series of cash flows. It is a standard method for using the time value of money to appraise long-term projects. Used for capital budgeting, and widely throughout economics, it measures the excess or shortfall of cash flows, in present value terms, once financing charges are met.

a. Tax shield
b. Net present value
c. Negative gearing
d. Present value of costs

3. _____ is the value on a given date of a future payment or series of future payments, discounted to reflect the time value of money and other factors such as investment risk. _____ calculations are widely used in business and economics to provide a means to compare cash flows at different times on a meaningful 'like to like' basis.

The most commonly applied model of the time value of money is compound interest.

a. Present value of benefits
b. Net present value
c. Negative gearing
d. Present value

4. _____ is the removal or simplification of government rules and regulations that constrain the operation of market forces. _____ does not mean elimination of laws against fraud, but eliminating or reducing government control of how business is done, thereby moving toward a more free market.

The stated rationale for '_____' is often that fewer and simpler regulations will lead to a raised level of competitiveness, therefore higher productivity, more efficiency and lower prices overall.

- a. Supply shock
- b. Demand shock
- c. Value added
- d. Deregulation

5. In finance, the _____ is the global financial market for short-term borrowing and lending. It provides short-term liquidity funding for the global financial system. The _____ is where short-term obligations such as Treasury bills, commercial paper and bankers' acceptances are bought and sold.
- a. Cramdown
- b. Money market
- c. Consumer debt
- d. Debt-for-equity swap

6. _____, in bookkeeping, refers to assets, liabilities, income, and expenses recorded on individual pages of the so called book of final entry or ledger. Changes in _____ value are made by chronologically posting debit (DR) and credit (CR) entries to its page. Examples of _____s are cash, _____s receivable, mortgages, loans, land and buildings, common stock, sales, services provided, wages, and payroll overhead.
- a. Account
- b. Alpha
- c. Option
- d. Accretion

7. A _____ is a current account at a banking institution that allows money to be deposited and withdrawn by the account holder, with the transactions and resulting balance being recorded on the bank's books. Some banks charge a fee for this service, while others may pay the customer interest on the funds deposited.

Although restrictions placed on access depend upon the terms and conditions of the account and the provider, the account holder retains rights to have their funds repaid on demand.

- a. Bilateral netting
- b. Deposit account
- c. 4-4-5 Calendar
- d. Contractum trinius

8. A _____ is a system (including physical or electronic infrastructure and associated procedures and protocols) used to settle financial transactions in bond markets, currency markets, and futures, derivatives or options markets, or to transfer funds between financial institutions. Due to the backing of modern fiat currencies with government bonds, _____s are a core part of modern monetary systems.
- a. 7-Eleven
- b. 529 plan
- c. 4-4-5 Calendar
- d. Payment system

9.

A _____ is a type of financial intermediary and a type of bank. Commercial banking is also known as business banking. It is a bank that provides checking accounts, savings accounts, and money market accounts and that accepts time deposits.

- a. 529 plan
- b. 4-4-5 Calendar
- c. Commercial bank
- d. 7-Eleven

Chapter 8. The Payment System and Financial Institution Relationships

10. _____ is the provision of resources (such as granting a loan) by one party to another party where that second party does not reimburse the first party immediately, thereby generating a debt, and instead arranges either to repay or return those resources (or material(s) of equal value) at a later date. The first party is called a creditor, also known as a lender, while the second party is called a debtor, also known as a borrower.

Movements of financial capital are normally dependent on either _____ or equity transfers.

a. Clearing house
b. Comparable
c. Warrant
d. Credit

11. A _____ is a cooperative financial institution that is owned and controlled by its members, and operated for the purpose of promoting thrift, providing credit at reasonable rates, and providing other financial services to its members. Many _____s exist to further community development or sustainable international development on a local level. Worldwide, _____ systems vary significantly in terms of total system assets and average institution asset size since _____s exist in a wide range of sizes, ranging from volunteer operations with a handful of members to institutions with several billion dollars in assets and hundreds of thousands of members.

a. Fi-linx
b. Credit union
c. Credit Union Service Organization
d. Corporate credit union

12. The _____ of 1982 (Pub.L. 97-320, H.R. 6267, enacted 1982-10-15) is an Act of Congress, that deregulated the Savings and Loan industry. This Act turned out to be one of many contributing factors that led to the Savings and Loan crisis of the late 1980s.

a. Garn-St. Germain Depository Institutions Act
b. Public Utility Holding Company Act
c. 4-4-5 Calendar
d. 529 plan

13. In financial accounting, the term _____ is most commonly used to describe any part of shareholders' equity, except for basic share capital. Sometimes, the term is used instead of the term provision; such a use, however, is inconsistent with the terminology suggested by International Accounting Standards Board. For more information about provisions, see provision (accounting.)

a. Treasury stock
b. Closing entries
c. FIFO and LIFO accounting
d. Reserve

14. The _____ of 1956 (12 U.S.C. § 1841, et seq.) is a United States Act of Congress that regulates the actions of bank holding companies.

The original law (subsequently amended), specified that the Federal Reserve Board of Governors must approve the establishment of a bank holding company, and prohibited bank holding companies headquartered in one state from acquiring a bank in another state. The law was implemented in part to regulate and control banks that had formed bank holding companies in order to own both banking and non-banking businesses.

a. Truth in Lending Act
b. Fair Credit Reporting Act
c. Bank Holding Company Act
d. Fair Credit Billing Act

15. _____ refer to services provided by the finance industry.

The finance industry encompasses a broad range of organizations that deal with the management of money. Among these organizations are banks, credit card companies, insurance companies, consumer finance companies, stock brokerages, investment funds and some government sponsored enterprises.

a. Delta hedging
b. Cost of carry
c. Financial instruments
d. Financial Services

16. The _____ Act is an Act of the 106th United States Congress which repealed part of the Glass-Steagall Act of 1933, opening up competition among banks, securities companies and insurance companies. The Glass-Steagall Act prohibited any one institution from acting as both an investment bank and a commercial bank, or as both a bank and an insurer.

The _____ Act (GLBA) allowed commercial and investment banks to consolidate.

a. 7-Eleven
b. 529 plan
c. Gramm-Leach-Bliley
d. 4-4-5 Calendar

17. A _____ is a company that owns other companies' outstanding stock. It usually refers to a company which does not produce goods or services itself, rather its only purpose is owning shares of other companies. They allow the reduction of risk for the owners and can allow the ownership and control of a number of different companies.

a. MRU Holdings
b. Federal National Mortgage Association
c. Privately held company
d. Holding Company

18. The _____ is a United States federal law enacted in 1927 from recommendations made by the comptroller of the currency Henry May Dawes.

The Act sought to give national banks competitive equality with state-chartered banks by letting national banks branch to the extent permitted by state law. The _____ specifically prohibited interstate branching by allowing each national bank to branch only within the state in which it is situated.

a. McFadden Act
b. Business valuation
c. Duty of loyalty
d. Covenant

19. In United States banking, _____ is a marketing term for certain services offered primarily to larger business customers. It may be used to describe all bank accounts (such as checking accounts) provided to businesses of a certain size, but it is more often used to describe specific services such as cash concentration, zero balance accounting, and automated clearing house facilities. Sometimes, private banking customers are given _____ services.

a. Global tactical asset allocation
b. Capitalization rate
c. Profitability index
d. Cash management

20. The institution most often referenced by the word '_____' is a public or publicly traded _____, the shares of which are traded on a public stock exchange (e.g., the New York Stock Exchange or Nasdaq in the United States) where shares of stock of _____s are bought and sold by and to the general public. Most of the largest businesses in the world are publicly traded _____s. However, the majority of _____s are said to be closely held, privately held or close _____s, meaning that no ready market exists for the trading of shares.

Chapter 8. The Payment System and Financial Institution Relationships

a. Corporation
b. Depository Trust Company
c. Federal Home Loan Mortgage Corporation
d. Protect

21. Explicit _____ is a measure implemented in many countries to protect bank depositors, in full or in part, from losses caused by a bank's inability to pay its debts when due. _____ systems are one component of a financial system safety net that promotes financial stability.
   a. Deposit Insurance
   b. Time deposit
   c. Reserve requirement
   d. Banking panic

22. The _____ is a United States government corporation created by the Glass-Steagall Act of 1933. It provides deposit insurance, which guarantees the safety of checking and savings deposits in member banks, currently up to $250,000 per depositor per bank. Insured deposits are backed by the full faith and credit of the United States.
   a. NYSE Group
   b. Federal Deposit Insurance Corporation
   c. Ford Foundation
   d. FASB

23. The _____ of 1991, passed during the Savings and loan crisis, strengthened the power of the Federal Deposit Insurance Corporation.

It allowed the FDIC to borrow directly from the Treasury department and mandated that the FDIC resolve failed banks using the least-costly method available. It also ordered the FDIC to assess insurance premiums according to risk and created new capital requirements.

   a. Federal Deposit Insurance Corporation Improvement Act
   b. Covenant
   c. National Securities Markets Improvement Act of 1996
   d. Fair Debt Collection Practices Act

24. The _____ , a component of the Federal Reserve System, is charged under United States law with overseeing the nation's open market operations. It is the Federal Reserve Committee that makes key decisions about interest rates and the growth jam of the United States money supply. It is the principal organ of United States national monetary policy.
   a. Federal Open Market Committee
   b. Tax incidence
   c. Fiscal policy
   d. Tax exemption

25. A _____, reserve bank, or monetary authority is the entity responsible for the monetary policy of a country or of a group of member states. It is a bank that can lend money to other banks in times of need. Its primary responsibility is to maintain the stability of the national currency and money supply, but more active duties include controlling subsidized-loan interest rates, and acting as a lender of last resort to the banking sector during times of financial crisis (private banks often being integral to the national financial system.)
   a. 529 plan
   b. 4-4-5 Calendar
   c. 7-Eleven
   d. Central bank

26. In banking and finance, _____ denotes all activities from the time a commitment is made for a transaction until it is settled. _____ is necessary because the speed of trades is much faster than the cycle time for completing the underlying transaction.

In its widest sense _____ involves the management of post-trading, pre-settlement credit exposures, to ensure that trades are settled in accordance with market rules, even if a buyer or seller should become insolvent prior to settlement.

a. Clearing house
b. Clearing
c. Procter ' Gamble
d. Share

27. A _____ is a financial services company that provides clearing and settlement services for financial transactions, usually on a futures exchange, and often acts as central counterparty (the payor actually pays the _____, which then pays the payee). A _____ may also offer novation, the substitution of a new contract or debt for an old, or other credit enhancement services to its members.

The term is also used for banks like Suffolk Bank that acted as a restraint on the over-issuance of private bank notes.

a. Valuation
b. Clearing house
c. Bucket shop
d. Warrant

28. The _____ is a private, not-for-profit organization whose primary purpose is to develop generally accepted accounting principles (GAAP) within the United States in the public's interest. The Securities and Exchange Commission (SEC) designated the _____ as the organization responsible for setting accounting standards for public companies in the U.S. It was created in 1973, replacing the Accounting Principles Board and the Committee on Accounting Procedure of the American Institute of Certified Public Accountants. The _____'s mission is 'to establish and improve standards of financial accounting and reporting for the guidance and education of the public, including issuers, auditors, and users of financial information.'

The _____ is not a governmental body.

a. PlaNet Finance
b. MRU Holdings
c. FASB
d. Credit karma

29. _____ is a type of bank account where the money in the account is legally able to be withdrawn immediately upon demand (or 'at call'.) This type of bank account can also be referred to as a 'cheque' or 'checking' or transactional account.

This type of bank account, allowing immediate conversion of the account balance into cash or withdrawal to another account, can be contrasted with a time deposit (also known as a certificate of deposit or term deposit), where the funds are not legally available for immediate withdrawal by the depositor.

a. Synthetic lease
b. 4-4-5 Calendar
c. 529 plan
d. Demand deposit

30. The _____ was enacted in 1987 by the United States Congress for the purpose of standardizing hold periods on deposits made to commercial banks and to regulate institutions' use of deposit holds. It is also referred to as Regulation CC or Reg CC, after the Federal Reserve regulation that implements the act. The law is codified in Title 12, Chapter 41 of the US Code and Title 12, Part 229 of the Code of Federal Regulations.

Chapter 8. The Payment System and Financial Institution Relationships

a. A Random Walk Down Wall Street
b. Expedited Funds Availability Act
c. ABN Amro
d. AAB

31. A _____ is the principal book for recording transactions. Originally, the term referred to a large volume of Scripture/service book kept in one place in church and accessible.

According to Charles Wriothesley's Chronicle (1538):

> the curates should provide a booke of the bible in Englishe, of the largest volume, to be a lidger in the same church for the parishioners to read on.

It is an application of this original meaning that is found in the commercial usage of the term for the principal book of account in a business house, the general _____ or nominal _____ and also in the terms purchase _____ and sales _____.

a. General journal
b. General ledger
c. Journal entry
d. Ledger

32. A _____ can require immediate payment by the second party to the third upon presentation of the _____. This is called a sight _____. A Cheques is a sight _____. An importer might write a _____ promising payment to an exporter for delivery of goods with payment to occur 60 days after the goods are delivered. Such a _____ is called a time _____.

a. Gross profit margin
b. Draft
c. Cashflow matching
d. Second lien loan

33. In finance, a _____ is a security that entitles the holder to buy stock of the company that issued it at a specified price, which is usually higher than the stock price at time of issue.

_____s are frequently attached to bonds or preferred stock as a sweetener, allowing the issuer to pay lower interest rates or dividends. They can be used to enhance the yield of the bond, and make them more attractive to potential buyers.

a. Warrant
b. Credit
c. Clearing
d. Clearing house

34. _____ is one of a series of accounting transactions dealing with the billing of customers who owe money to a person, company or organization for goods and services that have been provided to the customer. In most business entities this is typically done by generating an invoice and mailing or electronically delivering it to the customer, who in turn must pay it within an established timeframe called credit or payment terms.

An example of a common payment term is Net 30, meaning payment is due in the amount of the invoice 30 days from the date of invoice.

a. Accounting methods
c. Accounts receivable
b. Income
d. Impaired asset

35. _____ is a file or account that contains money that a person or company owes to suppliers, but hasn't paid yet (a form of debt.) When you receive an invoice you add it to the file, and then you remove it when you pay. Thus, the A/P is a form of credit that suppliers offer to their purchasers by allowing them to pay for a product or service after it has already been received.
   a. Outstanding balance
   c. Accounts payable
   b. Accrual
   d. Earnings before interest, taxes, depreciation and amortization

36. In economics, business, and accounting, a _____ is the value of money that has been used up to produce something, and hence is not available for use anymore. In business, the _____ may be one of acquisition, in which case the amount of money expended to acquire it is counted as _____. In this case, money is the input that is gone in order to acquire the thing.
   a. Sliding scale fees
   c. Marginal cost
   b. Fixed costs
   d. Cost

37. _____ or economic opportunity loss is the value of the next best alternative foregone as the result of making a decision. _____ analysis is an important part of a company's decision-making processes but is not treated as an actual cost in any financial statement. The next best thing that a person can engage in is referred to as the _____ of doing the best thing and ignoring the next best thing to be done.
   a. A Random Walk Down Wall Street
   c. ABN Amro
   b. AAB
   d. Opportunity cost

38. In finance, the _____ is the system that allows the transfer of money between savers and borrowers.

Put another way: the _____ is a set of complex and closely interconnected financial institutions, markets, instruments, services, practices, and transactions.

   a. 4-4-5 Calendar
   c. Passive income
   b. Horizontal merger
   d. Financial system

39. _____ or amalgamation is the act of merging many things into one. In business, it often refers to the mergers or acquisitions of many smaller companies into much larger ones. The financial accounting term of _____ refers to the aggregated financial statements of a group company as consolidated account.
   a. Retained earnings
   c. Write-off
   b. Cost of goods sold
   d. Consolidation

40. _____ is one of the oldest financial services firms in the world. It is a leader in financial services with assets of $2.3 trillion., and the largest market capitalization and deposit base of any U.S. banking institution.
   a. Comanity
   c. Double-declining-balance method
   b. JPMorgan Chase ' Co.
   d. Weighted mean

Chapter 9. Cash Collection Systems

1. _____ is the balance of the amounts of cash being received and paid by a business during a defined period of time, sometimes tied to a specific project. Measurement of _____ can be used

   - to evaluate the state or performance of a business or project.
   - to determine problems with liquidity. Being profitable does not necessarily mean being liquid. A company can fail because of a shortage of cash, even while profitable.
   - to generate project rate of returns. The time of _____s into and out of projects are used as inputs to financial models such as internal rate of return, and net present value.
   - to examine income or growth of a business when it is believed that accrual accounting concepts do not represent economic realities. Alternately, _____ can be used to 'validate' the net income generated by accrual accounting.

   _____ as a generic term may be used differently depending on context, and certain _____ definitions may be adapted by analysts and users for their own uses. Common terms include operating _____ and free _____.

   _____s can be classified into:

   1. Operational _____s: Cash received or expended as a result of the company's core business activities.
   2. Investment _____s: Cash received or expended through capital expenditure, investments or acquisitions.
   3. Financing _____s: Cash received or expended as a result of financial activities, such as interests and dividends.

   All three together - the net _____ - are necessary to reconcile the beginning cash balance to the ending cash balance. Loan draw downs or equity injections, that is just shifting of capital but no expenditure as such, are not considered in the net _____.

   a. Corporate finance
   c. Cash flow
   b. Shareholder value
   d. Real option

2. A _____ is a business that pursues payments on debts owed by individuals or businesses. Most collection agencies operate as agents of creditors and collect debts for a fee or percentage of the total amount owed. Some agencies, sometimes referred to as 'debt buyers', purchase debts from creditors for a fraction of the value of the debt and pursue the debtor for the full balance.
   a. Partial Payment
   c. Collection agency
   b. Guaranteed consumer funding
   d. Commercial hard money

3. The free _____ of a public company is an estimate of the proportion of shares that are not held by large owners and that are not stock with sales restrictions (restricted stock that cannot be sold until they become unrestricted stock.)

Chapter 9. Cash Collection Systems

The free _____ or a public _____ is usually defined as being all shares held by investors other than:

- shares held by owners owning more than 5% of all shares (those could be institutional investors, 'strategic shareholders,' founders, executives, and other insiders' holdings)
- restricted stocks (granted to executives that can be, but don't have to be, registered insiders)
- insider holdings (it is assumed that insiders hold stock for the very long term)

The free _____ is an important criterion in quoting a share on the stock market.

To _____ a company means to list its shares on a public stock exchange through an initial public offering (or 'flotation'.)

- Open market
- Outstanding shares
- Market capitalization
- Public _____ *loat*
- Reverse takeover

a. Golden parachute
c. Trade finance
b. Synthetic CDO
d. Float

4. In economics, business, and accounting, a _____ is the value of money that has been used up to produce something, and hence is not available for use anymore. In business, the _____ may be one of acquisition, in which case the amount of money expended to acquire it is counted as _____. In this case, money is the input that is gone in order to acquire the thing.

a. Marginal cost
c. Fixed costs
b. Sliding scale fees
d. Cost

5. The _____ is an expected return that the provider of capital plans to earn on their investment.

Capital (money) used for funding a business should earn returns for the capital providers who risk their capital. For an investment to be worthwhile, the expected return on capital must be greater than the _____.

a. Capital intensity
c. 4-4-5 Calendar
b. Cost of capital
d. Weighted average cost of capital

6. _____ is the process of dispersing decision-making governance closer to the people or citizen. It includes the dispersal of administration or governance in sectors or areas like engineering, management science, political science, political economy, sociology and economics. _____ is also possible in the dispersal of population and employment.

a. Corporate Transparency
c. Cash cow
b. Decentralization
d. Management by exception

Chapter 9. Cash Collection Systems

7. The institution most often referenced by the word '_____' is a public or publicly traded _____, the shares of which are traded on a public stock exchange (e.g., the New York Stock Exchange or Nasdaq in the United States) where shares of stock of _____s are bought and sold by and to the general public. Most of the largest businesses in the world are publicly traded _____s. However, the majority of _____s are said to be closely held, privately held or close _____s, meaning that no ready market exists for the trading of shares.
   a. Depository Trust Company
   b. Corporation
   c. Protect
   d. Federal Home Loan Mortgage Corporation

8. _____ consists of the sale of goods or merchandise from a fixed location, such as a department store, boutique or kiosk in small or individual lots for direct consumption by the purchaser. _____ may include subordinated services, such as delivery. Purchasers may be individuals or businesses.
   a. 529 plan
   b. 4-4-5 Calendar
   c. 7-Eleven
   d. Retailing

9. A _____ is a letter sent by a customer to a supplier, to inform that supplier that their invoice has been paid. If the customer is paying by cheque, the _____ often accompanies the cheque.

   _____s are not mandatory, however they are seen as a courtesy because they help the supplier's accounts department to match invoices with payments.

   a. Fixed asset
   b. Remittance advice
   c. Petty cash
   d. Construction in Progress

10. A _____ is an association of two or more individuals, companies, organizations or governments (or any combination of these entities) with the objective of participating in a common activity or pooling their resources for achieving a common goal.
    a. Consortium
    b. 529 plan
    c. 4-4-5 Calendar
    d. 7-Eleven

11. _____ is one of the oldest financial services firms in the world. It is a leader in financial services with assets of $2.3 trillion., and the largest market capitalization and deposit base of any U.S. banking institution.
    a. JPMorgan Chase ' Co.
    b. Weighted mean
    c. Double-declining-balance method
    d. Comanity

12. In mathematics, _____ is a technique for optimization of a linear objective function, subject to linear equality and linear inequality constraints. Informally, _____ determines the way to achieve the best outcome (such as maximum profit or lowest cost) in a given mathematical model and given some list of requirements represented as linear equations.

More formally, given a polytope (for example, a polygon or a polyhedron), and a real-valued affine function

defined on this polytope, a _____ method will find a point in the polytope where this function has the smallest (or largest) value.

a. 529 plan	b. 4-4-5 Calendar
c. 7-Eleven	d. Linear programming

Chapter 10. Cash Concentration

1. A _____ is a financial services company that provides clearing and settlement services for financial transactions, usually on a futures exchange, and often acts as central counterparty (the payor actually pays the _____, which then pays the payee). A _____ may also offer novation, the substitution of a new contract or debt for an old, or other credit enhancement services to its members.

The term is also used for banks like Suffolk Bank that acted as a restraint on the over-issuance of private bank notes.

a. Warrant
c. Clearing house
b. Bucket shop
d. Valuation

2. _____ is the process of dispersing decision-making governance closer to the people or citizen. It includes the dispersal of administration or governance in sectors or areas like engineering, management science, political science, political economy, sociology and economics. _____ is also possible in the dispersal of population and employment.

a. Decentralization
c. Cash cow
b. Corporate Transparency
d. Management by exception

3. In economics, business, and accounting, a _____ is the value of money that has been used up to produce something, and hence is not available for use anymore. In business, the _____ may be one of acquisition, in which case the amount of money expended to acquire it is counted as _____. In this case, money is the input that is gone in order to acquire the thing.

a. Sliding scale fees
c. Marginal cost
b. Cost
d. Fixed costs

4. The _____ is an expected return that the provider of capital plans to earn on their investment.

Capital (money) used for funding a business should earn returns for the capital providers who risk their capital. For an investment to be worthwhile, the expected return on capital must be greater than the _____.

a. 4-4-5 Calendar
c. Capital intensity
b. Cost of capital
d. Weighted average cost of capital

5. _____, in microeconomics, are the cost advantages that a business obtains due to expansion. _____ may be utilized by any size firm expanding its scale of operation.

a. Economies of scale
c. Employee Retirement Income Security Act
b. Articles of incorporation
d. Uniform Commercial Code

6. _____ or economic opportunity loss is the value of the next best alternative foregone as the result of making a decision. _____ analysis is an important part of a company's decision-making processes but is not treated as an actual cost in any financial statement. The next best thing that a person can engage in is referred to as the _____ of doing the best thing and ignoring the next best thing to be done.

a. ABN Amro
c. AAB
b. A Random Walk Down Wall Street
d. Opportunity cost

Chapter 10. Cash Concentration

7. _____ is the transfer of funds from diverse accounts into a central account to improve the efficiency of cash management. The consolidation of cash into a single account allows a company to maintain smaller cash balances overall, and to identify excess cash available for short term investments. The cash available in different bank accounts are pooled into a master account. The advantages of _____ are 1) Cash control 2) Cash visibility .

  a. Cash concentration   b. Capitalization rate
  c. Conditional prepayment rate   d. Profitability index

8. _____ is the balance of the amounts of cash being received and paid by a business during a defined period of time, sometimes tied to a specific project. Measurement of _____ can be used

- to evaluate the state or performance of a business or project.
- to determine problems with liquidity. Being profitable does not necessarily mean being liquid. A company can fail because of a shortage of cash, even while profitable.
- to generate project rate of returns. The time of _____s into and out of projects are used as inputs to financial models such as internal rate of return, and net present value.
- to examine income or growth of a business when it is believed that accrual accounting concepts do not represent economic realities. Alternately, _____ can be used to 'validate' the net income generated by accrual accounting.

_____ as a generic term may be used differently depending on context, and certain _____ definitions may be adapted by analysts and users for their own uses. Common terms include operating _____ and free _____.

_____s can be classified into:

1. Operational _____s: Cash received or expended as a result of the company's core business activities.
2. Investment _____s: Cash received or expended through capital expenditure, investments or acquisitions.
3. Financing _____s: Cash received or expended as a result of financial activities, such as interests and dividends.

All three together - the net _____ - are necessary to reconcile the beginning cash balance to the ending cash balance. Loan draw downs or equity injections, that is just shifting of capital but no expenditure as such, are not considered in the net _____.

  a. Cash flow   b. Shareholder value
  c. Corporate finance   d. Real option

9. _____ are horizontal lines drawn on an statistical process control chart, usually at a distance of $>\pm 3$ standard deviations of the plotted statistic from the statistic's mean.

For normally distributed statistics, the area bracketed by the _____ will on average contain 99.73% of all the plot points on the chart, as long as the process is and remains in statistical control.

_____ should not be confused with tolerance limits, which are completely independent of the distribution of the plotted sample statistic.

Chapter 10. Cash Concentration

a. 4-4-5 Calendar
b. Control limits
c. 529 plan
d. 7-Eleven

10. In accountancy, _____ is a company's average collection period. A low number of days indicates that the company collects its outstanding receivables quickly. Typically, _____ is calculated monthly. The _____ figure is an index of the relationship between outstanding receivables and sales achieved over a given period. The _____ analysis provides general information about the number of days on average that customers take to pay invoices.
   a. Days sales outstanding
   b. Net pay
   c. Residual value
   d. Round-tripping

11. _____ is a financial metric which represents operating liquidity available to a business. Along with fixed assets such as plant and equipment, _____ is considered a part of operating capital. It is calculated as current assets minus current liabilities.
   a. 529 plan
   b. 4-4-5 Calendar
   c. Working capital management
   d. Working capital

12. In mathematics, _____ is a technique for optimization of a linear objective function, subject to linear equality and linear inequality constraints. Informally, _____ determines the way to achieve the best outcome (such as maximum profit or lowest cost) in a given mathematical model and given some list of requirements represented as linear equations.

More formally, given a polytope (for example, a polygon or a polyhedron), and a real-valued affine function

defined on this polytope, a _____ method will find a point in the polytope where this function has the smallest (or largest) value.

   a. 529 plan
   b. 4-4-5 Calendar
   c. 7-Eleven
   d. Linear programming

Chapter 11. Cash Disbursement Systems

1. _____ is the balance of the amounts of cash being received and paid by a business during a defined period of time, sometimes tied to a specific project. Measurement of _____ can be used

   - to evaluate the state or performance of a business or project.
   - to determine problems with liquidity. Being profitable does not necessarily mean being liquid. A company can fail because of a shortage of cash, even while profitable.
   - to generate project rate of returns. The time of _____s into and out of projects are used as inputs to financial models such as internal rate of return, and net present value.
   - to examine income or growth of a business when it is believed that accrual accounting concepts do not represent economic realities. Alternately, _____ can be used to 'validate' the net income generated by accrual accounting.

_____ as a generic term may be used differently depending on context, and certain _____ definitions may be adapted by analysts and users for their own uses. Common terms include operating _____ and free _____.

_____s can be classified into:

1. Operational _____s: Cash received or expended as a result of the company's core business activities.
2. Investment _____s: Cash received or expended through capital expenditure, investments or acquisitions.
3. Financing _____s: Cash received or expended as a result of financial activities, such as interests and dividends.

All three together - the net _____ - are necessary to reconcile the beginning cash balance to the ending cash balance. Loan draw downs or equity injections, that is just shifting of capital but no expenditure as such, are not considered in the net _____.

   a. Real option
   b. Corporate finance
   c. Shareholder value
   d. Cash flow

2. The free _____ of a public company is an estimate of the proportion of shares that are not held by large owners and that are not stock with sales restrictions (restricted stock that cannot be sold until they become unrestricted stock.)

The free _____ or a public _____ is usually defined as being all shares held by investors other than:

   - shares held by owners owning more than 5% of all shares (those could be institutional investors, 'strategic shareholders,' founders, executives, and other insiders' holdings)
   - restricted stocks (granted to executives that can be, but don't have to be, registered insiders)
   - insider holdings (it is assumed that insiders hold stock for the very long term)

The free _____ is an important criterion in quoting a share on the stock market.

Chapter 11. Cash Disbursement Systems 47

To _____ a company means to list its shares on a public stock exchange through an initial public offering (or 'flotation'.)

- Open market
- Outstanding shares
- Market capitalization
- Public _____ *loat*
- Reverse takeover

a. Golden parachute   b. Synthetic CDO
c. Trade finance   d. Float

3. In banking and finance, _____ denotes all activities from the time a commitment is made for a transaction until it is settled. _____ is necessary because the speed of trades is much faster than the cycle time for completing the underlying transaction.

In its widest sense _____ involves the management of post-trading, pre-settlement credit exposures, to ensure that trades are settled in accordance with market rules, even if a buyer or seller should become insolvent prior to settlement.

a. Clearing house   b. Procter ' Gamble
c. Share   d. Clearing

4. A _____ is a financial services company that provides clearing and settlement services for financial transactions, usually on a futures exchange, and often acts as central counterparty (the payor actually pays the _____, which then pays the payee). A _____ may also offer novation, the substitution of a new contract or debt for an old, or other credit enhancement services to its members.

The term is also used for banks like Suffolk Bank that acted as a restraint on the over-issuance of private bank notes.

a. Warrant   b. Bucket shop
c. Clearing House   d. Valuation

5. A _____ is a system (including physical or electronic infrastructure and associated procedures and protocols) used to settle financial transactions in bond markets, currency markets, and futures, derivatives or options markets, or to transfer funds between financial institutions. Due to the backing of modern fiat currencies with government bonds, _____s are a core part of modern monetary systems.

a. 7-Eleven   b. 529 plan
c. 4-4-5 Calendar   d. Payment system

Chapter 11. Cash Disbursement Systems

6. _____ is the provision of resources (such as granting a loan) by one party to another party where that second party does not reimburse the first party immediately, thereby generating a debt, and instead arranges either to repay or return those resources (or material(s) of equal value) at a later date. The first party is called a creditor, also known as a lender, while the second party is called a debtor, also known as a borrower.

Movements of financial capital are normally dependent on either _____ or equity transfers.

   a. Clearing house   b. Credit
   c. Warrant   d. Comparable

7. _____ is the process of dispersing decision-making governance closer to the people or citizen. It includes the dispersal of administration or governance in sectors or areas like engineering, management science, political science, political economy, sociology and economics. _____ is also possible in the dispersal of population and employment.

   a. Corporate Transparency   b. Management by exception
   c. Cash cow   d. Decentralization

8. _____, in bookkeeping, refers to assets, liabilities, income, and expenses recorded on individual pages of the so called book of final entry or ledger. Changes in _____ value are made by chronologically posting debit (DR) and credit (CR) entries to its page. Examples of _____s are cash, _____s receivable, mortgages, loans, land and buildings, common stock, sales, services provided, wages, and payroll overhead.

   a. Option   b. Accretion
   c. Alpha   d. Account

9. _____ is the difference between price and the costs of bringing to market whatever it is that is accounted as an enterprise (whether by harvest, extraction, manufacture, or purchase) in terms of the component costs of delivered goods and/or services and any operating or other expenses.

A key difficulty in measuring profit is in defining costs. Pure economic monetary profits can be zero or negative even in competitive equilibrium when accounted monetized costs exceed monetized price.

   a. Accounting profit   b. AAB
   c. A Random Walk Down Wall Street   d. Economic profit

10. _____ or financing is to provide capital (funds), which means money for a project, a person, a business or any other private or public institutions.

Those funds can be allocated for either short term or long term purposes. The health fund is a new way of _____ private healthcare centers.

   a. Proxy fight   b. Synthetic CDO
   c. Product life cycle   d. Funding

11. In corporate finance, _____ is an estimate of true economic profit after making corrective adjustments to GAAP accounting, including deducting the opportunity cost of equity capital. GAAP is estimated to ignore US$300 billion in shareholder opportunity costs. _____ can be measured as Net Operating Profit After Taxes(or NOPAT) less the money cost of capital.

a. ABN Amro
b. AAB
c. A Random Walk Down Wall Street
d. Economic value added

12. _____ refers to the additional value of a commodity over the cost of commodities used to produce it from the previous stage of production. An example is the price of gasoline at the pump over the price of the oil in it. In national accounts used in macroeconomics, it refers to the contribution of the factors of production, i.e., land, labor, and capital goods, to raising the value of a product and corresponds to the incomes received by the owners of these factors.
a. Value added
b. Deregulation
c. Demand shock
d. Supply shock

13. _____ is subcontracting a process, such as product design or manufacturing, to a third-party company. The decision to outsource is often made in the interest of lowering cost or making better use of time and energy costs, redirecting or conserving energy directed at the competencies of a particular business, or to make more efficient use of land, labor, capital, (information) technology and resources. _____ became part of the business lexicon during the 1980s.
a. Exchange Rate Mechanism
b. AT'T Inc.
c. OTC Bulletin Board
d. Outsourcing

14. _____ or net present worth (NPW) is defined as the total present value (PV) of a time series of cash flows. It is a standard method for using the time value of money to appraise long-term projects. Used for capital budgeting, and widely throughout economics, it measures the excess or shortfall of cash flows, in present value terms, once financing charges are met.
a. Negative gearing
b. Present value of costs
c. Tax shield
d. Net present value

15. _____ is the value on a given date of a future payment or series of future payments, discounted to reflect the time value of money and other factors such as investment risk. _____ calculations are widely used in business and economics to provide a means to compare cash flows at different times on a meaningful 'like to like' basis.

The most commonly applied model of the time value of money is compound interest.

a. Net present value
b. Negative gearing
c. Present value of benefits
d. Present value

16. _____ is a legally enforceable arrangement between a bank and a counterparty that creates a single legal obligation covering all included individual contracts. This means that a bank'e;s obligation, in the event of the default or insolvency of one of the parties, would be the net sum of all positive and negative fair values of contracts included in the _____ arrangement.
a. 4-4-5 Calendar
b. Contractum trinius
c. Bilateral netting
d. Deposit account

17. _____ refers to the likelihood that changes in the business environment adversely affect operating profits or the value of assets in a specific country. For example, financial factors such as currency controls, devaluation or regulatory changes, or stability factors such as mass riots, civil war and other potential events contribute to companies' operational risks. This term is also sometimes referred to as political risk, however _____ is a more general term, which generally only refers to risks affecting all companies operating within a particular country.

Chapter 11. Cash Disbursement Systems

a. Solvency
b. Single-index model
c. Capital asset
d. Country risk

18. In general, _____ means to allow a positive value and a negative value to set-off and partially or entirely cancel each other out.

In the context of credit risk, there are at least three specific types of _____:

- Close-out _____

- _____ by novation

- Settlement or payment _____

_____ decreases credit exposure, increases business with existing counterparties, and reduces both operational and settlement risk and operational costs.

a. Reinvestment risk
b. Moneylender
c. Forward price
d. Netting

19. When companies conduct business across borders, they must deal in foreign currencies. Companies must exchange foreign currencies for home currencies when dealing with receivables, and vice versa for payables. This is done at the current exchange rate between the two countries. _____ is the risk that the exchange rate will change unfavorably before the currency is exchanged.

a. Lower of cost or market rule
b. 529 plan
c. 4-4-5 Calendar
d. Foreign exchange risk

Chapter 12. Cash Forecasting

1. _____ is the balance of the amounts of cash being received and paid by a business during a defined period of time, sometimes tied to a specific project. Measurement of _____ can be used

   - to evaluate the state or performance of a business or project.
   - to determine problems with liquidity. Being profitable does not necessarily mean being liquid. A company can fail because of a shortage of cash, even while profitable.
   - to generate project rate of returns. The time of _____s into and out of projects are used as inputs to financial models such as internal rate of return, and net present value.
   - to examine income or growth of a business when it is believed that accrual accounting concepts do not represent economic realities. Alternately, _____ can be used to 'validate' the net income generated by accrual accounting.

   _____ as a generic term may be used differently depending on context, and certain _____ definitions may be adapted by analysts and users for their own uses. Common terms include operating _____ and free _____.

   _____s can be classified into:

   1. Operational _____s: Cash received or expended as a result of the company's core business activities.
   2. Investment _____s: Cash received or expended through capital expenditure, investments or acquisitions.
   3. Financing _____s: Cash received or expended as a result of financial activities, such as interests and dividends.

   All three together - the net _____ - are necessary to reconcile the beginning cash balance to the ending cash balance. Loan draw downs or equity injections, that is just shifting of capital but no expenditure as such, are not considered in the net _____.

   a. Real option
   c. Cash flow
   b. Shareholder value
   d. Corporate finance

2. A _____ is a pool of assets forming an independent legal entity that are bought with the contributions to a pension plan for the exclusive purpose of financing pension plan benefits.

   _____s are important shareholders of listed and private companies. They are especially important to the stock market where large institutional investors like the Ontario Teachers' Pension Plan dominate.

   a. Limited liability company
   c. Leveraged buyout
   b. Pension fund
   d. Leverage

3. Working capital requirements of a business should be monitored at all times to ensure that there are sufficient funds available to meet short-term expenses.

   The _____ is basically a detailed plan that shows all expected sources and uses of cash

a. Mitigating Control
c. Rate of return
b. Loans and interest, in Judaism
d. Cash budget

4. _____ is concerned with the tasks of developing and applying quantitative or statistical methods to the study and elucidation of economic principles. _____ combines economic theory with statistics to analyze and test economic relationships. Theoretical _____ considers questions about the statistical properties of estimators and tests, while applied _____ is concerned with the application of econometric methods to assess economic theories.
   a. ABN Amro
   c. A Random Walk Down Wall Street
   b. Econometrics
   d. AAB

5. In probability theory and statistics, the _____ of a random variable, probability distribution averaging the squared distance of its possible values from the expected value (mean.) Whereas the mean is a way to describe the location of a distribution, the _____ is a way to capture its scale or degree of being spread out. The unit of _____ is the square of the unit of the original variable.
   a. Variance
   c. Monte Carlo methods
   b. Semivariance
   d. Harmonic mean

6. _____ is the difference between price and the costs of bringing to market whatever it is that is accounted as an enterprise (whether by harvest, extraction, manufacture, or purchase) in terms of the component costs of delivered goods and/or services and any operating or other expenses.

A key difficulty in measuring profit is in defining costs. Pure economic monetary profits can be zero or negative even in competitive equilibrium when accounted monetized costs exceed monetized price.

   a. A Random Walk Down Wall Street
   c. Economic profit
   b. AAB
   d. Accounting profit

7. Accrual, in accounting, describes the accounting method known as _____, whereby revenues and expenses are recognized when they are accrued, i.e. accumulated (earned or incurred), regardless when the actual cash is received or paid out.

E.g. a company delivers a product to a customer who will pay for it 30 days later in the next fiscal year starting a week after the delivery. The company recognizes the proceeds as a revenue in its current income statement still for the fiscal year of the delivery, even though it will get paid in cash during the following accounting period.

   a. A Random Walk Down Wall Street
   c. Accrual basis
   b. ABN Amro
   d. AAB

8. In financial accounting, a _____ or statement of financial position is a summary of a person's or organization's balances. Assets, liabilities and ownership equity are listed as of a specific date, such as the end of its financial year. A _____ is often described as a snapshot of a company's financial condition.
   a. Financial statements
   c. Statement on Auditing Standards No. 70: Service Organizations
   b. Statement of retained earnings
   d. Balance sheet

9. The term _____ is a term applied to practices that are perfunctory, or seek to satisfy the minimum requirements or to conform to a convention or doctrine. It has different meanings in different fields.

In accounting, _____ earnings are those earnings of companies in addition to actual earnings calculated under the Generally Accepted Accounting Principles (GAAP) in their quarterly and yearly financial reports.

a. Deferred financing costs
b. Pro forma
c. Long-term liabilities
d. Deferred income

10. The _____ (NYSE: FRE) is an insolvent government sponsored enterprise (GSE) of the United States federal government.

The _____ was created in 1970 to expand the secondary market for mortgages in the US. Along with other GSEs, Freddie Mac buys mortgages on the secondary market, pools them, and sells them as mortgage-backed securities to investors on the open market.

a. Federal Home Loan Mortgage Corporation
b. Public company
c. The Depository Trust ' Clearing Corporation
d. Governmental Accounting Standards Board

11. _____ is possibly the most important step in the model building sequence. It is also one of the most overlooked. Often the validation of a model seems to consist of nothing more than quoting the R^2 statistic from the fit (which measures the fraction of the total variability in the response that is accounted for by the model).

a. Model validation
b. 529 plan
c. 7-Eleven
d. 4-4-5 Calendar

12. In financial accounting, the term _____ is most commonly used to describe any part of shareholders' equity, except for basic share capital. Sometimes, the term is used instead of the term provision; such a use, however, is inconsistent with the terminology suggested by International Accounting Standards Board. For more information about provisions, see provision (accounting.)

a. Treasury stock
b. FIFO and LIFO accounting
c. Closing entries
d. Reserve

13. A _____, reserve bank, or monetary authority is the entity responsible for the monetary policy of a country or of a group of member states. It is a bank that can lend money to other banks in times of need. Its primary responsibility is to maintain the stability of the national currency and money supply, but more active duties include controlling subsidized-loan interest rates, and acting as a lender of last resort to the banking sector during times of financial crisis (private banks often being integral to the national financial system.)

a. 4-4-5 Calendar
b. Central bank
c. 7-Eleven
d. 529 plan

14. _____ is the study of how the variation (uncertainty) in the output of a mathematical model can be apportioned, qualitatively or quantitatively, to different sources of variation in the input of a model .

In more general terms uncertainty and sensitivity analyses investigate the robustness of a study when the study includes some form of mathematical modelling. While uncertainty analysis studies the overall uncertainty in the conclusions of the study, _____ tries to identify what source of uncertainty weights more on the study's conclusions.

a. Sensitivity analysis
b. Proxy fight
c. Synthetic CDO
d. Golden parachute

15. In statistics, a _____ is the difference between the actual or real and the predicted or forecast value of a time series or any other phenomenon of interest.

In simple cases, a forecast is compared with an outcome at a single time-point and a summary of _____s is constructed over a collection of such time-points. Here the forecast may be assessed using the difference or using a proportional error.

a. 4-4-5 Calendar
b. 529 plan
c. Forecast error
d. 7-Eleven

16. In statistics, _____ has two related meanings:

- the arithmetic _____
- the expected value of a random variable, which is also called the population _____.

It is sometimes stated that the '_____' is average. This is incorrect if '_____' is taken in the specific sense of 'arithmetic _____' as there are different types of averages: the _____, median, and mode. Other simple statistical analyses use measures of spread, such as range, interquartile range, or standard deviation. For a real-valued random variable X, the _____ is the expectation of X. Note that not every probability distribution has a defined _____; see the Cauchy distribution for an example.

a. Harmonic mean
b. Sample size
c. Mean
d. Probability distribution

17. In statistics, the _____ is a quantity used to measure how close forecasts or predictions are to the eventual outcomes. The _____ is given by

As the name suggests, the _____ is an average of the absolute errors $e_i = f_i >- y_i$, where f_i is the prediction and y_i the true value. Note that alternative formulations may include relative frequencies as weight factors.

a. 529 plan
b. 4-4-5 Calendar
c. Root mean square deviation
d. Mean absolute error

Chapter 12. Cash Forecasting

18. In statistics, the _____, R² is used in the context of statistical models whose main purpose is the prediction of future outcomes on the basis of other related information. It is the proportion of variability in a data set that is accounted for by the statistical model. It provides a measure of how well future outcomes are likely to be predicted by the model.
    a. 4-4-5 Calendar
    b. Coefficient of determination
    c. 7-Eleven
    d. 529 plan

19. In statistics, the _____ or _____ of an estimator is one of many ways to quantify the amount by which an estimator differs from the true value of the quantity being estimated. As a loss function, _____ is called squared error loss. _____ measures the average of the square of the 'error.' The error is the amount by which the estimator differs from the quantity to be estimated.
    a. Mean squared error
    b. 4-4-5 Calendar
    c. Root mean square deviation
    d. 529 plan

20. The _____ (also root mean square error (RMSE)) is a frequently-used measure of the differences between values predicted by a model or an estimator and the values actually observed from the thing being modeled or estimated. _____ is a good measure of accuracy. These individual differences are also called residuals, and the _____ serves to aggregate them into a single measure of predictive power.
    a. Mean squared error
    b. 4-4-5 Calendar
    c. Root mean square deviation
    d. 529 plan

21. In statistics, _____ is used for two things;

    - to construct a simple formula that will predict a value or values for a variable given the value of another variable.
    - to test whether and how a given variable is related to another variable or variables.

    _____ is a form of regression analysis in which the relationship between one or more independent variables and another variable, called the dependent variable, is modelled by a least squares function, called a _____ equation. This function is a linear combination of one or more model parameters, called regression coefficients. A _____ equation with one independent variable represents a straight line when the predicted value (i.e. the dependant variable from the regression equation) is plotted against the independent variable: this is called a simple _____. However, note that 'linear' does not refer to this straight line, but rather to the way in which the regression coefficients occur in the regression equation.

    a. Foreign Language and Area Studies
    b. Stock trader
    c. Wall Street Crash of 1929
    d. Linear regression

22. In statistics, _____ is a technique that can be applied to time series data, either to produce smoothed data for presentation, or to make forecasts. The time series data themselves are a sequence of observations. The observed phenomenon may be an essentially random process, or it may be an orderly, but noisy, process.
    a. ABN Amro
    b. AAB
    c. Exponential smoothing
    d. A Random Walk Down Wall Street

23. _____ is defined by APICS as a method for the effective planning of all resources of a manufacturing company. Ideally, it addresses operational planning in units, financial planning in dollars, and has a simulation capability to answer 'what-if' questions and extension of closed-loop _____. Manufacturing Resource Planning - Around 1980, over-frequent changes in sales forecasts, entailing continual readjustments in production, as well as the unsuitability of the parameters fixed by the system, led _____ to evolve into a new concept : _____.

This is not exclusively a software function, but a marriage of people skills, dedication to data base accuracy, and computer resources.

a. 7-Eleven
b. 4-4-5 Calendar
c. Manufacturing resource planning
d. 529 plan

24. In statistics, a _____, is a type of finite impulse response filter used to analyze a set of data points by creating a series of averages of different subsets of the full data set. A _____ is not a single number, but it is a set of numbers, each of which is the average of the corresponding subset of a larger set of data points. A _____ may also use unequal weights for each data value in the subset to emphasize particular values in the subset.

a. Moving average
b. Voluntary Emissions Reductions
c. Gordon growth model
d. Loans and interest, in Judaism

25. In statistics and image processing, to smooth a data set is to create an approximating function that attempts to capture important patterns in the data, while leaving out noise or other fine-scale structures/rapid phenomena. Many different algorithms are used in _____. One of the most common algorithms is the 'moving average', often used to try to capture important trends in repeated statistical surveys.

a. 7-Eleven
b. 529 plan
c. 4-4-5 Calendar
d. Smoothing

26. In statistics, a _____ is a mathematical relationship in which two occurrences have no causal connection, yet it may be inferred that they do, due to a certain third, unseen factor (referred to as a 'confounding factor' or 'lurking variable'.) The _____ gives an impression of a worthy link between two groups that is invalid when objectively examined.

The misleading correlation between two variables is produced through the operation of a third causal variable.

a. 529 plan
b. Spurious relationship
c. 4-4-5 Calendar
d. 7-Eleven

27. In probability theory and statistics, _____ indicates the strength and direction of a linear relationship between two random variables. That is in contrast with the usage of the term in colloquial speech, which denotes any relationship, not necessarily linear. In general statistical usage, _____ or co-relation refers to the departure of two random variables from independence.

a. Geometric mean
b. Probability distribution
c. Correlation
d. Variance

28. _____ (or spoilage) refers to the process by which tissues of dead organisms break down into simpler forms of matter. Such a breakdown of dead organisms is essential for new growth and development of living organisms because it recycles the finite chemical constituents and frees up the limited physical space in the biome. Bodies of living organisms begin to decompose shortly after death.

a. 4-4-5 Calendar
b. 7-Eleven
c. 529 plan
d. Decomposition

Chapter 13. Short-Term Financial Planning

1. _____ is the balance of the amounts of cash being received and paid by a business during a defined period of time, sometimes tied to a specific project. Measurement of _____ can be used

- to evaluate the state or performance of a business or project.
- to determine problems with liquidity. Being profitable does not necessarily mean being liquid. A company can fail because of a shortage of cash, even while profitable.
- to generate project rate of returns. The time of _____s into and out of projects are used as inputs to financial models such as internal rate of return, and net present value.
- to examine income or growth of a business when it is believed that accrual accounting concepts do not represent economic realities. Alternately, _____ can be used to 'validate' the net income generated by accrual accounting.

_____ as a generic term may be used differently depending on context, and certain _____ definitions may be adapted by analysts and users for their own uses. Common terms include operating _____ and free _____.

_____s can be classified into:

1. Operational _____s: Cash received or expended as a result of the company's core business activities.
2. Investment _____s: Cash received or expended through capital expenditure, investments or acquisitions.
3. Financing _____s: Cash received or expended as a result of financial activities, such as interests and dividends.

All three together - the net _____ - are necessary to reconcile the beginning cash balance to the ending cash balance. Loan draw downs or equity injections, that is just shifting of capital but no expenditure as such, are not considered in the net _____.

 a. Corporate finance   b. Cash flow
 c. Shareholder value   d. Real option

2. _____ is the task of determining how a business will afford to achieve its strategic goals and objectives. Usually, a company creates a Financial Plan immediately after the vision and objectives have been set. The Financial Plan describes each of the activities, resources, equipment and materials that are needed to achieve these objectives, as well as the timeframes involved.
 a. Corporate Transparency   b. Performance measurement
 c. Financial planning   d. Management by exception

3. In economics, the concept of the _____ refers to the decision-making time frame of a firm in which at least one factor of production is fixed. Costs which are fixed in the _____ have no impact on a firms decisions. For example a firm can raise output by increasing the amount of labour through overtime.
 a. Long-run   b. 529 plan
 c. 4-4-5 Calendar   d. Short-run

4. In general usage, a _____ can be a budget, a plan for spending and saving future income. This plan allocates future income to various types of expenses, such as rent or utilities, and also reserves some income for short-term and long-term savings. A _____ can also be an investment plan, which allocates savings to various assets or projects expected to produce future income, such as a new business or product line, shares in an existing business, or real estate.

Chapter 13. Short-Term Financial Planning

a. Title loan
b. Promissory note
c. Credit repair software
d. Financial plan

5. _____, refers to consumption opportunity gained by an entity within a specified time frame, which is generally expressed in monetary terms. However, for households and individuals, '_____ is the sum of all the wages, salaries, profits, interests payments, rents and other forms of earnings received... in a given period of time.' For firms, _____ generally refers to net-profit: what remains of revenue after expenses have been subtracted.

a. Accrual
b. Annual report
c. OIBDA
d. Income

6. _____ is a fee paid on borrowed assets. It is the price paid for the use of borrowed money, or, money earned by deposited funds. Assets that are sometimes lent with _____ include money, shares, consumer goods through hire purchase, major assets such as aircraft, and even entire factories in finance lease arrangements.

a. AAB
b. Insolvency
c. A Random Walk Down Wall Street
d. Interest

7. The institution most often referenced by the word '_____' is a public or publicly traded _____, the shares of which are traded on a public stock exchange (e.g., the New York Stock Exchange or Nasdaq in the United States) where shares of stock of _____s are bought and sold by and to the general public. Most of the largest businesses in the world are publicly traded _____s. However, the majority of _____s are said to be closely held, privately held or close _____s, meaning that no ready market exists for the trading of shares.

a. Corporation
b. Protect
c. Federal Home Loan Mortgage Corporation
d. Depository Trust Company

Chapter 14. The Money Market

1. The institution most often referenced by the word '_____' is a public or publicly traded _____, the shares of which are traded on a public stock exchange (e.g., the New York Stock Exchange or Nasdaq in the United States) where shares of stock of _____s are bought and sold by and to the general public. Most of the largest businesses in the world are publicly traded _____s. However, the majority of _____s are said to be closely held, privately held or close _____s, meaning that no ready market exists for the trading of shares.
   a. Depository Trust Company
   b. Protect
   c. Federal Home Loan Mortgage Corporation
   d. Corporation

2. _____ is a life of security. It may also refer to the final payment date of a loan or other financial instrument, at which point all remaining interest and principal is due to be paid.

   1, 3, 6 months _____ band can be calculated by using 30-day per month periods.

   a. Primary market
   b. False billing
   c. Replacement cost
   d. Maturity

3. In finance, the _____ is the global financial market for short-term borrowing and lending. It provides short-term liquidity funding for the global financial system. The _____ is where short-term obligations such as Treasury bills, commercial paper and bankers' acceptances are bought and sold.
   a. Consumer debt
   b. Cramdown
   c. Debt-for-equity swap
   d. Money market

4. The _____ is that part of the capital markets that deals with the issuance of new securities. Companies, governments or public sector institutions can obtain funding through the sale of a new stock or bond issue. This is typically done through a syndicate of securities dealers.
   a. Sector rotation
   b. Volatility clustering
   c. Primary market
   d. Peer group analysis

5. _____ consists of the sale of goods or merchandise from a fixed location, such as a department store, boutique or kiosk in small or individual lots for direct consumption by the purchaser. _____ may include subordinated services, such as delivery. Purchasers may be individuals or businesses.
   a. 529 plan
   b. 4-4-5 Calendar
   c. 7-Eleven
   d. Retailing

6. The _____ is the financial market where previously issued securities and financial instruments such as stock, bonds, options, and futures are bought and sold. The term '_____' is also used refer to the market for any used goods or assets, or an alternative use for an existing product or asset where the customer base is the second market

   With primary issuances of securities or financial instruments, or the primary market, investors purchase these securities directly from issuers such as corporations issuing shares in an IPO or private placement, or directly from the federal government in the case of treasuries.

   a. Delta neutral
   b. Secondary market
   c. Financial market
   d. Performance attribution

Chapter 14. The Money Market

7. _____ is a fee paid on borrowed assets. It is the price paid for the use of borrowed money, or, money earned by deposited funds. Assets that are sometimes lent with _____ include money, shares, consumer goods through hire purchase, major assets such as aircraft, and even entire factories in finance lease arrangements.
   a. AAB
   b. A Random Walk Down Wall Street
   c. Interest
   d. Insolvency

8. An _____ is the price a borrower pays for the use of money they do not own, and the return a lender receives for deferring the use of funds, by lending it to the borrower. _____s are normally expressed as a percentage rate over the period of one year.

   _____s targets are also a vital tool of monetary policy and are used to control variables like investment, inflation, and unemployment.

   a. ABN Amro
   b. Interest rate
   c. A Random Walk Down Wall Street
   d. AAB

9. In financial accounting, the term _____ is most commonly used to describe any part of shareholders' equity, except for basic share capital. Sometimes, the term is used instead of the term provision; such a use, however, is inconsistent with the terminology suggested by International Accounting Standards Board. For more information about provisions, see provision (accounting.)
   a. FIFO and LIFO accounting
   b. Treasury stock
   c. Closing entries
   d. Reserve

10. In economics, the concept of the _____ refers to the decision-making time frame of a firm in which at least one factor of production is fixed. Costs which are fixed in the _____ have no impact on a firms decisions. For example a firm can raise output by increasing the amount of labour through overtime.
    a. 4-4-5 Calendar
    b. Long-run
    c. 529 plan
    d. Short-run

11. In probability theory and statistics, _____ indicates the strength and direction of a linear relationship between two random variables. That is in contrast with the usage of the term in colloquial speech, which denotes any relationship, not necessarily linear. In general statistical usage, _____ or co-relation refers to the departure of two random variables from independence.
    a. Variance
    b. Probability distribution
    c. Geometric mean
    d. Correlation

12. A _____ s a time deposit, a financial product commonly offered to consumers by banks, thrift institutions, and credit unions.

    They are similar to savings accounts in that they are insured and thus virtually risk-free; they are 'money in the bank'. They are different from savings accounts in that they have a specific, fixed term (often three months, six months, or one to five years), and, usually, a fixed interest rate.

    a. Reserve requirement
    b. Certificate of deposit
    c. Variable rate mortgage
    d. Time deposit

Chapter 14. The Money Market

13. _____ is a measure of the ability of a debtor to pay their debts as and when they fall due. It is usually expressed as a ratio or a percentage of current liabilities.

For a corporation with a published balance sheet there are various ratios used to calculate a measure of liquidity.

a. Operating profit margin
b. Invested capital
c. Operating leverage
d. Accounting liquidity

14. _____ arises from situations in which a party interested in trading an asset cannot do it because nobody in the market wants to trade that asset. _____ becomes particularly important to parties who are about to hold or currently hold an asset, since it affects their ability to trade.

Manifestation of _____ is very different from a drop of price to zero.

a. Liquidity risk
b. Currency risk
c. Credit risk
d. Tracking error

15. A _____ is a money deposit at a banking institution that cannot be withdrawn for a certain 'term' or period of time. When the term is over it can be withdrawn or it can be held for another term. Generally speaking, the longer the term the better the yield on the money.

a. Basel Accord
b. Time deposit
c. Certificate of deposit
d. Private money

16. In finance, 'participation' is an ownership interest in a mortgage or other loan. In particular, _____ is a cooperation of multiple lenders to issue a loan (known as participation loan) to one borrower. This is usually done in order to reduce individual risks of the lenders.

a. Securitization
b. Loan participation
c. Short positions
d. Doctrine of the Proper Law

17. _____ is a structured finance process that involves pooling and repackaging of cash-flow-producing financial assets into securities, which are then sold to investors. The term '_____' is derived from the fact that the form of financial instruments used to obtain funds from the investors are securities. As a portfolio risk backed by amortizing cash flows - and unlike general corporate debt - the credit quality of securitized debt is non-stationary due to changes in volatility that are time- and structure-dependent.

a. Special journals
b. Reputational risk
c. The Glass-Steagall Act of 1933
d. Securitization

18. In business and accounting, _____s are everything of value that is owned by a person or company. The balance sheet of a firm records the monetary value of the _____s owned by the firm. The two major _____ classes are tangible _____s and intangible _____s.

a. EBITDA
b. Asset
c. Income
d. Accounts payable

Chapter 14. The Money Market

19. In the global money market, _____ is an unsecured promissory note with a fixed maturity of one to 270 days. _____ is a money-market security issued (sold) by large banks and corporations to get money to meet short term debt obligations (for example, payroll), and is only backed by an issuing bank or corporation's promise to pay the face amount on the maturity date specified on the note. Since it is not backed by collateral, only firms with excellent credit ratings from a recognized rating agency will be able to sell their _____ at a reasonable price.
    a. Book building
    b. Financial distress
    c. Commercial paper
    d. Trade-off theory

20. A _____ is a fungible, negotiable instrument representing financial value. They are broadly categorized into debt securities (such as banknotes, bonds and debentures), and equity securities; e.g., common stocks. The company or other entity issuing the _____ is called the issuer.
    a. Tracking stock
    b. Securities lending
    c. Security
    d. Book entry

21. The U.S. _____ is an independent agency of the United States government which holds primary responsibility for enforcing the federal securities laws and regulating the securities industry, the nation's stock and options exchanges, and other electronic securities markets. The SEC was created by section 4 of the SEC of 1934 (now codified as 15 U.S.C. Â§ 78d and commonly referred to as the 1934 Act.)
    a. 4-4-5 Calendar
    b. 529 plan
    c. 7-Eleven
    d. Securities and Exchange Commission

22. _____ is typically a higher ranking stock than voting shares, and its terms are negotiated between the corporation and the investor.

    _____ usually carry no voting rights, but may carry superior priority over common stock in the payment of dividends and upon liquidation. _____ may carry a dividend that is paid out prior to any dividends to common stock holders.

    a. Second lien loan
    b. Follow-on offering
    c. Trade-off theory
    d. Preferred stock

23. In finance, the term _____ describes the amount in cash that returns to the owners of a security. Normally it does not include the price variations, at the difference of the total return. _____ applies to various stated rates of return on stocks (common and preferred, and convertible), fixed income instruments (bonds, notes, bills, strips, zero coupon), and some other investment type insurance products (e.g. annuities.)
    a. 4-4-5 Calendar
    b. Yield to maturity
    c. Macaulay duration
    d. Yield

24. A _____ is a payment made by a corporation to its shareholder members. When a corporation earns a profit or surplus, that money can be put to two uses: it can either be re-invested in the business (called retained earnings), or it can be paid to the shareholders as a _____. Many corporations retain a portion of their earnings and pay the remainder as a _____.
    a. Dividend puzzle
    b. Dividend
    c. Dividend yield
    d. Special dividend

Chapter 14. The Money Market

25. The _____ on a company stock is the company's annual dividend payments divided by its market cap, or the dividend per share divided by the price per share. It is often expressed as a percentage.

Dividend payments on preferred shares are stipulated by the prospectus.

- a. Dividend imputation
- b. Special dividend
- c. Dividend reinvestment plan
- d. Dividend yield

26. _____ are government bonds issued by the United States Department of the Treasury through the Bureau of the Public Debt. They are the debt financing instruments of the U.S. Federal government, and they are often referred to simply as Treasuries or Treasurys. There are four types of marketable _____: Treasury bills, Treasury notes, Treasury bonds, and Treasury Inflation Protected Securities (TIPS.)

- a. 4-4-5 Calendar
- b. Treasury Inflation-Protected Securities
- c. Treasury Inflation Protected Securities
- d. Treasury securities

27. _____ is the provision of resources (such as granting a loan) by one party to another party where that second party does not reimburse the first party immediately, thereby generating a debt, and instead arranges either to repay or return those resources (or material(s) of equal value) at a later date. The first party is called a creditor, also known as a lender, while the second party is called a debtor, also known as a borrower.

Movements of financial capital are normally dependent on either _____ or equity transfers.

- a. Credit
- b. Warrant
- c. Clearing house
- d. Comparable

28. The _____ provide stable, on-demand, low-cost funding to American financial institutions for home mortgage loans, small business, rural, agricultural, and economic development lending. With their members, the _____ank System represents the largest collective source of home mortgage and community credit in the United States. The banks do not provide loans directly to individuals, only to other banks.

- a. Federal Home Loan Banks
- b. 529 plan
- c. 4-4-5 Calendar
- d. 7-Eleven

29. The _____ (NYSE: FRE) is an insolvent government sponsored enterprise (GSE) of the United States federal government.

The _____ was created in 1970 to expand the secondary market for mortgages in the US. Along with other GSEs, Freddie Mac buys mortgages on the secondary market, pools them, and sells them as mortgage-backed securities to investors on the open market.

- a. Federal Home Loan Mortgage Corporation
- b. Public company
- c. Governmental Accounting Standards Board
- d. The Depository Trust ' Clearing Corporation

30. The _____ (NYSE: FNM), commonly known as Fannie Mae, is a stockholder-owned corporation chartered by Congress in 1968 as a government sponsored enterprise (GSE), but founded in 1938 during the Great Depression. The corporation's purpose is to purchase and securitize mortgages in order to ensure that funds are consistently available to the institutions that lend money to home buyers.

Chapter 14. The Money Market

On September 7, 2008, James Lockhart, director of the Federal Housing Finance Agency (FHFA), announced that Fannie Mae and Freddie Mac were being placed into conservatorship of the FHFA.

a. The Depository Trust ' Clearing Corporation
b. SPDR
c. General partnership
d. Federal National Mortgage Association

31. The _____ is a U.S. government-owned corporation within the Department of Housing and Urban Development

Ginnie Mae provides guarantees on mortgage-backed securities backed by federally insured or guaranteed loans, mainly loans issued by the Federal Housing Administration, Department of Veterans Affairs, Rural Housing Service, and Office of Public and Indian Housing. Ginnie Mae securities are the only MBS that are guaranteed by the United States government.

a. 4-4-5 Calendar
b. Graduated payment mortgage
c. Jumbo mortgage
d. Government National Mortgage Association

32. A _____ is a legal pledge in United States municipal finance, in which an entity pledges its full faith and credit to repay its debt, typically a _____ bond.

a. Financial Institutions Reform Recovery and Enforcement Act
b. General obligation
c. Letter of credit
d. Covenant

33. A _____ is a professionally managed type of collective investment scheme that pools money from many investors and invests it in stocks, bonds, short-term money market instruments, and/or other securities. The _____ will have a fund manager that trades the pooled money on a regular basis. Currently, the worldwide value of all _____s totals more than $26 trillion.

Since 1940, there have been three basic types of investment companies in the United States: open-end funds, also known in the US as _____s; unit investment trusts (UITs); and closed-end funds.

a. Net asset value
b. Mutual fund
c. Financial intermediary
d. Trust company

34. In business, _____ is income that a company receives from its normal business activities, usually from the sale of goods and services to customers. Some companies also receive _____ from interest, dividends or royalties paid to them by other companies. _____ may refer to business income in general, or it may refer to the amount, in a monetary unit, received during a period of time, as in 'Last year, Company X had _____ of $32 million.'

In many countries, including the UK, _____ is referred to as turnover.

a. Matching principle
b. Furniture, Fixtures and Equipment
c. Revenue
d. Bottom line

Chapter 14. The Money Market

35. A _____ allows a borrower to use a financial security as collateral for a cash loan at a fixed rate of interest. In a repo, the borrower agrees to immediately sell a security to a lender and also agrees to buy the same security from the lender at a fixed price at some later date. A repo is equivalent to a cash transaction combined with a forward contract.
   a. Repurchase agreement
   b. Total return swap
   c. Contango
   d. Volatility arbitrage

36. _____, in bookkeeping, refers to assets, liabilities, income, and expenses recorded on individual pages of the so called book of final entry or ledger. Changes in _____ value are made by chronologically posting debit (DR) and credit (CR) entries to its page. Examples of _____s are cash, _____s receivable, mortgages, loans, land and buildings, common stock, sales, services provided, wages, and payroll overhead.
   a. Option
   b. Alpha
   c. Accretion
   d. Account

37. A '_____' is a 'Charge' that is paid to obtain the right to delay a payment. Essentially, the payer purchases the right to make a given payment in the future instead of in the Present. The '_____', or 'Charge' that must be paid to delay the payment, is simply the difference between what the payment amount would be if it were paid in the present and what the payment amount would be paid if it were paid in the future.
   a. Value at risk
   b. Risk aversion
   c. Risk modeling
   d. Discount

38. In finance, the yield curve is the relation between the interest rate (or cost of borrowing) and the time to maturity of the debt for a given borrower in a given currency. For example, the current U.S. dollar interest rates paid on U.S. Treasury securities for various maturities are closely watched by many traders, and are commonly plotted on a graph such as the one on the right which is informally called 'the yield curve.' More formal mathematical descriptions of this relation are often called the _____.

The yield of a debt instrument is the annualized percentage increase in the value of the investment.

   a. Term structure of interest rates
   b. 7-Eleven
   c. 529 plan
   d. 4-4-5 Calendar

39. In finance, the _____ is the relation between the interest rate (or cost of borrowing) and the time to maturity of the debt for a given borrower in a given currency. For example, the current U.S. dollar interest rates paid on U.S. Treasury securities for various maturities are closely watched by many traders, and are commonly plotted on a graph such as the one on the right which is informally called 'the _____.' More formal mathematical descriptions of this relation are often called the term structure of interest rates.

The yield of a debt instrument is the annualized percentage increase in the value of the investment.

   a. 4-4-5 Calendar
   b. 7-Eleven
   c. Yield curve
   d. 529 plan

40. The _____ or forward rate is the agreed upon price of an asset in a forward contract. Using the rational pricing assumption, we can express the _____ in terms of the spot price and any dividends etc., so that there is no possibility for arbitrage.

Chapter 14. The Money Market

The _____ is given by:

$$$$

where

F is the _____ to be paid at time T
e^x is the exponential function
r is the risk-free interest rate
q is the cost-of-carry
S_0 is the spot price of the asset (i.e. what it would sell for at time 0)
D_i is a dividend which is guaranteed to be paid at time t_i where $0 < t_i < T$.

The two questions here are what price the short position (the seller of the asset) should offer to maximize his gain, and what price the long position (the buyer of the asset) should accept to maximize his gain?

At the very least we know that both do not want to lose any money in the deal.

a. Security interest
b. Biweekly Mortgage
c. Forward price
d. Financial Gerontology

41. The _____ of a commodity, a security or a currency is the price that is quoted for immediate (spot) settlement (payment and delivery.) Spot settlement is normally one or two business days from trade date. This is in contrast with the forward price established in a forward contract or futures contract, where contract terms (price) are set now, but delivery and payment will occur at a future date.
   a. Limits to arbitrage
   b. Long position
   c. Market anomaly
   d. Spot rate

42. John Maynard Keynes developed the _____ of Interest in the General Theory of Employment Interest and Money. The primary consideration of the _____ is the demand for money as an asset, as a means for holding wealth. Interest rates, he argues, cannot be a reward for savings as such because, if a person hoards his savings in cash, keeping it under his mattress say, he will receive no interest, although he has nevertheless, refrained from consuming all his current income.
   a. Liquidity preference
   b. 7-Eleven
   c. 529 plan
   d. 4-4-5 Calendar

43. _____ is the corporate management term for the act of reorganizing the legal, ownership, operational, or other structures of a company for the purpose of making it more profitable or better organized for its present needs. Alternate reasons for restructing include a change of ownership or ownership structure, demerger repositioning debt _____ and financial _____.
   a. Concentrated stock
   b. Cross-border leasing
   c. Restructuring
   d. Day trading

Chapter 14. The Money Market

44. The _____ , a component of the Federal Reserve System, is charged under United States law with overseeing the nation's open market operations. It is the Federal Reserve Committee that makes key decisions about interest rates and the growth jam of the United States money supply. It is the principal organ of United States national monetary policy.
   a. Federal Open Market Committee
   b. Tax incidence
   c. Fiscal policy
   d. Tax exemption

45. In finance, the _____ is the difference between the quoted rates of return on two different investments, usually of different credit quality.

It is a compound of yield and spread.

The '_____ of X over Y' is simply the percentage return on investment (ROI) from financial instrument X minus the percentage return on investment from financial instrument Y (per annum.)

   a. Duty of loyalty
   b. Debtor-in-possession financing
   c. Portfolio insurance
   d. Yield spread

46. A _____ assesses the credit worthiness of an individual, corporation, or even a country. _____s are calculated from financial history and current assets and liabilities. Typically, a _____ tells a lender or investor the probability of the subject being able to pay back a loan.
   a. Credit cycle
   b. Credit report monitoring
   c. Debenture
   d. Credit rating

Chapter 15. Short-Term Investment Management

1. _____ is a fee paid on borrowed assets. It is the price paid for the use of borrowed money, or, money earned by deposited funds. Assets that are sometimes lent with _____ include money, shares, consumer goods through hire purchase, major assets such as aircraft, and even entire factories in finance lease arrangements.
   a. A Random Walk Down Wall Street
   b. Insolvency
   c. AAB
   d. Interest

2. An _____ is the price a borrower pays for the use of money they do not own, and the return a lender receives for deferring the use of funds, by lending it to the borrower. _____s are normally expressed as a percentage rate over the period of one year.

   _____s targets are also a vital tool of monetary policy and are used to control variables like investment, inflation, and unemployment.

   a. Interest rate
   b. ABN Amro
   c. AAB
   d. A Random Walk Down Wall Street

3. An _____ is any government regulation or law that encourages or discourages foreign investment in the local economy, e.g. currency exchange limits.

   As globalization integrates the economies of neighboring and of trading states, they are typically forced to trade off such rules as part of a common tax, tariff and trade regime, e.g. as defined by a free trade pact. _____ favoring local investors over global ones is typically discouraged in such pacts, and the idea of a separate _____ rapidly becomes a fiction or fantasy, as real decisions reflect the real need for nations to compete for investment, even from their own local investors.

   a. Investment policy
   b. ABN Amro
   c. A Random Walk Down Wall Street
   d. AAB

4. In economics, the concept of the _____ refers to the decision-making time frame of a firm in which at least one factor of production is fixed. Costs which are fixed in the _____ have no impact on a firms decisions. For example a firm can raise output by increasing the amount of labour through overtime.
   a. Long-run
   b. 4-4-5 Calendar
   c. 529 plan
   d. Short-run

5. _____ is normally any risk associated with any form of financing.

   Depending on the nature of the investment, the type of 'investment' risk will vary. High risk investments have greater potential rewards, but you may lose your money instead by taking the risk for more money.

   a. Revaluation
   b. Stock market index option
   c. Liquidating dividend
   d. Financial risk

6. A _____ is a fungible, negotiable instrument representing financial value. They are broadly categorized into debt securities (such as banknotes, bonds and debentures), and equity securities; e.g., common stocks. The company or other entity issuing the _____ is called the issuer.

Chapter 15. Short-Term Investment Management

a. Book entry
b. Tracking stock
c. Security
d. Securities lending

7. _____, in bookkeeping, refers to assets, liabilities, income, and expenses recorded on individual pages of the so called book of final entry or ledger. Changes in _____ value are made by chronologically posting debit (DR) and credit (CR) entries to its page. Examples of _____s are cash, _____s receivable, mortgages, loans, land and buildings, common stock, sales, services provided, wages, and payroll overhead.
a. Option
b. Alpha
c. Accretion
d. Account

8. _____ is one of a series of accounting transactions dealing with the billing of customers who owe money to a person, company or organization for goods and services that have been provided to the customer. In most business entities this is typically done by generating an invoice and mailing or electronically delivering it to the customer, who in turn must pay it within an established timeframe called credit or payment terms.

An example of a common payment term is Net 30, meaning payment is due in the amount of the invoice 30 days from the date of invoice.

a. Impaired asset
b. Accounts receivable
c. Income
d. Accounting methods

9. _____ is a list for goods and materials held available in stock by a business. It is also used for a list of the contents of a household and for a list for testamentary purposes of the possessions of someone who has died. In accounting _____ is considered an asset.
a. Inventory
b. AAB
c. A Random Walk Down Wall Street
d. ABN Amro

10. _____ is typically a higher ranking stock than voting shares, and its terms are negotiated between the corporation and the investor.

_____ usually carry no voting rights, but may carry superior priority over common stock in the payment of dividends and upon liquidation. _____ may carry a dividend that is paid out prior to any dividends to common stock holders.

a. Preferred stock
b. Second lien loan
c. Follow-on offering
d. Trade-off theory

11. _____ is a measure of the ability of a debtor to pay their debts as and when they fall due. It is usually expressed as a ratio or a percentage of current liabilities.

For a corporation with a published balance sheet there are various ratios used to calculate a measure of liquidity.

a. Operating profit margin
b. Invested capital
c. Operating leverage
d. Accounting liquidity

Chapter 15. Short-Term Investment Management

12. _____ is a file or account that contains money that a person or company owes to suppliers, but hasn't paid yet (a form of debt.) When you receive an invoice you add it to the file, and then you remove it when you pay. Thus, the A/P is a form of credit that suppliers offer to their purchasers by allowing them to pay for a product or service after it has already been received.
   a. Earnings before interest, taxes, depreciation and amortization
   b. Accrual
   c. Outstanding balance
   d. Accounts payable

13. A _____ is a variable associated with an increased risk of disease or infection. They are correlational and not necessarily causal, because correlation does not imply causation. For example, being young cannot be said to cause measles, but young people are more at risk as they are less likely to have developed immunity during a previous epidemic.
   a. 529 plan
   b. 7-Eleven
   c. 4-4-5 Calendar
   d. Risk factor

14. A _____ is a situation that involves losing one quality or aspect of something in return for gaining another quality or aspect. It implies a decision to be made with full comprehension of both the upside and downside of a particular choice.

   In economics the term is expressed as opportunity cost, referring the most preferred alternative given up.

   a. Trade-off
   b. Break-even point
   c. Total revenue
   d. Capital outflow

15. In statistics, the _____, R^2 is used in the context of statistical models whose main purpose is the prediction of future outcomes on the basis of other related information. It is the proportion of variability in a data set that is accounted for by the statistical model. It provides a measure of how well future outcomes are likely to be predicted by the model.
   a. 7-Eleven
   b. Coefficient of determination
   c. 529 plan
   d. 4-4-5 Calendar

16. In finance, the term _____ describes the amount in cash that returns to the owners of a security. Normally it does not include the price variations, at the difference of the total return. _____ applies to various stated rates of return on stocks (common and preferred, and convertible), fixed income instruments (bonds, notes, bills, strips, zero coupon), and some other investment type insurance products (e.g. annuities.)
   a. 4-4-5 Calendar
   b. Macaulay duration
   c. Yield to maturity
   d. Yield

17. In finance, the _____ is the difference between the quoted rates of return on two different investments, usually of different credit quality.

   It is a compound of yield and spread.

   The '_____ of X over Y' is simply the percentage return on investment (ROI) from financial instrument X minus the percentage return on investment from financial instrument Y (per annum.)

   a. Yield spread
   b. Debtor-in-possession financing
   c. Duty of loyalty
   d. Portfolio insurance

Chapter 15. Short-Term Investment Management

18. _____ refers to a portfolio management strategy where the manager makes specific investments with the goal of outperforming an investment benchmark index. Investors or mutual funds that do not aspire to create a return in excess of a benchmark index will often invest in an index fund that replicates as closely as possible the investment weighting and returns of that index; this is called passive management. _____ is the opposite of passive management, because in passive management the manager does not seek to outperform the benchmark index.

   a. AAB
   b. Active management
   c. A Random Walk Down Wall Street
   d. ABN Amro

19. The institution most often referenced by the word '_____' is a public or publicly traded _____, the shares of which are traded on a public stock exchange (e.g., the New York Stock Exchange or Nasdaq in the United States) where shares of stock of _____s are bought and sold by and to the general public. Most of the largest businesses in the world are publicly traded _____s. However, the majority of _____s are said to be closely held, privately held or close _____s, meaning that no ready market exists for the trading of shares.

   a. Corporation
   b. Federal Home Loan Mortgage Corporation
   c. Depository Trust Company
   d. Protect

20. The _____ (NYSE: FRE) is an insolvent government sponsored enterprise (GSE) of the United States federal government.

The _____ was created in 1970 to expand the secondary market for mortgages in the US. Along with other GSEs, Freddie Mac buys mortgages on the secondary market, pools them, and sells them as mortgage-backed securities to investors on the open market.

   a. Public company
   b. The Depository Trust ' Clearing Corporation
   c. Federal Home Loan Mortgage Corporation
   d. Governmental Accounting Standards Board

21. In finance, the _____ is the relation between the interest rate (or cost of borrowing) and the time to maturity of the debt for a given borrower in a given currency. For example, the current U.S. dollar interest rates paid on U.S. Treasury securities for various maturities are closely watched by many traders, and are commonly plotted on a graph such as the one on the right which is informally called 'the _____.' More formal mathematical descriptions of this relation are often called the term structure of interest rates.

The yield of a debt instrument is the annualized percentage increase in the value of the investment.

   a. Yield curve
   b. 4-4-5 Calendar
   c. 529 plan
   d. 7-Eleven

22. _____ is the study of how the variation (uncertainty) in the output of a mathematical model can be apportioned, qualitatively or quantitatively, to different sources of variation in the input of a model .

In more general terms uncertainty and sensitivity analyses investigate the robustness of a study when the study includes some form of mathematical modelling. While uncertainty analysis studies the overall uncertainty in the conclusions of the study, _____ tries to identify what source of uncertainty weights more on the study's conclusions.

Chapter 15. Short-Term Investment Management

a. Proxy fight
c. Golden parachute
b. Synthetic CDO
d. Sensitivity analysis

23. A _____ is a payment made by a corporation to its shareholder members. When a corporation earns a profit or surplus, that money can be put to two uses: it can either be re-invested in the business (called retained earnings), or it can be paid to the shareholders as a _____. Many corporations retain a portion of their earnings and pay the remainder as a _____.

a. Dividend
c. Special dividend
b. Dividend yield
d. Dividend puzzle

24. _____ is a life of security. It may also refer to the final payment date of a loan or other financial instrument, at which point all remaining interest and principal is due to be paid.

1, 3, 6 months _____ band can be calculated by using 30-day per month periods.

a. Primary market
c. False billing
b. Replacement cost
d. Maturity

25. In finance, a _____ is a derivative in which two counterparties agree to exchange one stream of cash flows against another stream. These streams are called the legs of the _____.

The cash flows are calculated over a notional principal amount, which is usually not exchanged between counterparties.

a. Local volatility
c. Volatility swap
b. Volatility arbitrage
d. Swap

26. In finance, a _____ is a predefined set of rules for making trading decisions.

Traders, investment firms and fund managers use a _____ to help make wiser investment decisions and help eliminate the emotional aspect of trading. A _____ is governed by a set of rules that do not deviate.

a. Regulation FD
c. Commodity Pool Operator
b. Tail risk
d. Trading strategy

27. In United States banking, _____ is a marketing term for certain services offered primarily to larger business customers. It may be used to describe all bank accounts (such as checking accounts) provided to businesses of a certain size, but it is more often used to describe specific services such as cash concentration, zero balance accounting, and automated clearing house facilities. Sometimes, private banking customers are given _____ services.

a. Global tactical asset allocation
c. Profitability index
b. Capitalization rate
d. Cash management

28. _____ are horizontal lines drawn on an statistical process control chart, usually at a distance of >±3 standard deviations of the plotted statistic from the statistic's mean.

For normally distributed statistics, the area bracketed by the _____ will on average contain 99.73% of all the plot points on the chart, as long as the process is and remains in statistical control.

_____ should not be confused with tolerance limits, which are completely independent of the distribution of the plotted sample statistic.

a. 529 plan
c. 7-Eleven
b. 4-4-5 Calendar
d. Control limits

Chapter 16. Short-Term Financing

1. _____ is a term applied in many countries to a reference interest rate used by banks. The term originally indicated the rate of interest at which banks lent to favored customers, i.e., those with high credibility, though this is no longer always the case. Some variable interest rates may be expressed as a percentage above or below _____.
    a. Prime rate
    b. Reserve requirement
    c. Credit bureau
    d. Time deposit

2. _____ is the balance of the amounts of cash being received and paid by a business during a defined period of time, sometimes tied to a specific project. Measurement of _____ can be used

    - to evaluate the state or performance of a business or project.
    - to determine problems with liquidity. Being profitable does not necessarily mean being liquid. A company can fail because of a shortage of cash, even while profitable.
    - to generate project rate of returns. The time of _____s into and out of projects are used as inputs to financial models such as internal rate of return, and net present value.
    - to examine income or growth of a business when it is believed that accrual accounting concepts do not represent economic realities. Alternately, _____ can be used to 'validate' the net income generated by accrual accounting.

    _____ as a generic term may be used differently depending on context, and certain _____ definitions may be adapted by analysts and users for their own uses. Common terms include operating _____ and free _____.

    _____s can be classified into:

    1. Operational _____s: Cash received or expended as a result of the company's core business activities.
    2. Investment _____s: Cash received or expended through capital expenditure, investments or acquisitions.
    3. Financing _____s: Cash received or expended as a result of financial activities, such as interests and dividends.

    All three together - the net _____ - are necessary to reconcile the beginning cash balance to the ending cash balance. Loan draw downs or equity injections, that is just shifting of capital but no expenditure as such, are not considered in the net _____.

    a. Shareholder value
    b. Real option
    c. Corporate finance
    d. Cash flow

3. _____ or financing is to provide capital (funds), which means money for a project, a person, a business or any other private or public institutions.

    Those funds can be allocated for either short term or long term purposes. The health fund is a new way of _____ private healthcare centers.

    a. Proxy fight
    b. Synthetic CDO
    c. Product life cycle
    d. Funding

4. In business and accounting, _____s are everything of value that is owned by a person or company. The balance sheet of a firm records the monetary value of the _____s owned by the firm. The two major _____ classes are tangible _____s and intangible _____s.

   a. EBITDA
   b. Accounts payable
   c. Income
   d. Asset

5. In accounting, a _____ is an asset on the balance sheet which is expected to be sold or otherwise used up in the near future, usually within one year, or one business cycle - whichever is longer. Typical _____s include cash, cash equivalents, accounts receivable, inventory, the portion of prepaid accounts which will be used within a year, and short-term investments.

On the balance sheet, assets will typically be classified into _____s and long-term assets.

   a. Current asset
   b. Write-off
   c. Long-term liabilities
   d. Historical cost

6. In economics, the concept of the _____ refers to the decision-making time frame of a firm in which at least one factor of production is fixed. Costs which are fixed in the _____ have no impact on a firms decisions. For example a firm can raise output by increasing the amount of labour through overtime.

   a. Long-run
   b. Short-run
   c. 4-4-5 Calendar
   d. 529 plan

7. _____ is the provision of resources (such as granting a loan) by one party to another party where that second party does not reimburse the first party immediately, thereby generating a debt, and instead arranges either to repay or return those resources (or material(s) of equal value) at a later date. The first party is called a creditor, also known as a lender, while the second party is called a debtor, also known as a borrower.

Movements of financial capital are normally dependent on either _____ or equity transfers.

   a. Warrant
   b. Credit
   c. Comparable
   d. Clearing house

8. A _____ is the maximum amount of credit that a financial institution or other lender will extend to a debtor for a particular line of credit. For example, the maximum that a credit card company will allow a card holder to borrow at any given point on a specific card.

This limit is based on a variety of factors ranging from an individual's ability to make interest payments, an organization's cashflow and/or ability to repay the principal, to the credit standards employed by the lender.

   a. 529 plan
   b. 7-Eleven
   c. 4-4-5 Calendar
   d. Credit limit

9. _____ is exchange of capital, goods, and services across international borders or territories. In most countries, it represents a significant share of gross domestic product (GDP.) While _____ has been present throughout much of history, its economic, social, and political importance has been on the rise in recent centuries.

Chapter 16. Short-Term Financing

a. OTC Bulletin Board
b. International Trade
c. Index number
d. United States Treasury security

10. A _____ is any credit facility extended to a business by a bank or financial institution. A _____ may take several forms such as cash credit, overdraft, demand loan, export packing credit, term loan, discounting or purchase of commercial bills etc. It is like an account that can readily be tapped into if the need arises or not touched at all and saved for emergencies.
    a. Debt-snowball method
    b. Cash credit
    c. Line of credit
    d. Default Notice

11. A standard, commercial _____ is a document issued mostly by a financial institution, used primarily in trade finance, which usually provides an irrevocable payment undertaking.

The _____ can also be the source of payment for a transaction, meaning that redeeming the _____ will pay an exporter. Letters of credit are used primarily in international trade transactions of significant value, for deals between a supplier in one country and a customer in another.

    a. Duty of loyalty
    b. McFadden Act
    c. Letter of credit
    d. Bond indenture

12. The institution most often referenced by the word '_____' is a public or publicly traded _____, the shares of which are traded on a public stock exchange (e.g., the New York Stock Exchange or Nasdaq in the United States) where shares of stock of _____s are bought and sold by and to the general public. Most of the largest businesses in the world are publicly traded _____s. However, the majority of _____s are said to be closely held, privately held or close _____s, meaning that no ready market exists for the trading of shares.
    a. Protect
    b. Depository Trust Company
    c. Corporation
    d. Federal Home Loan Mortgage Corporation

13. A _____ allows a borrower to use a financial security as collateral for a cash loan at a fixed rate of interest. In a repo, the borrower agrees to immediately sell a security to a lender and also agrees to buy the same security from the lender at a fixed price at some later date. A repo is equivalent to a cash transaction combined with a forward contract.
    a. Total return swap
    b. Repurchase agreement
    c. Volatility arbitrage
    d. Contango

14. In finance, a _____ is a debt security, in which the authorized issuer owes the holders a debt and, depending on the terms of the _____, is obliged to pay interest (the coupon) and/or to repay the principal at a later date, termed maturity.

Thus a _____ is a loan: the issuer is the borrower, the _____ holder is the lender, and the coupon is the interest. _____s provide the borrower with external funds to finance long-term investments, or, in the case of government _____s, to finance current expenditure.

    a. Catastrophe bonds
    b. Bond
    c. Puttable bond
    d. Convertible bond

15. In the global money market, _____ is an unsecured promissory note with a fixed maturity of one to 270 days. _____ is a money-market security issued (sold) by large banks and corporations to get money to meet short term debt obligations (for example, payroll), and is only backed by an issuing bank or corporation's promise to pay the face amount on the maturity date specified on the note. Since it is not backed by collateral, only firms with excellent credit ratings from a recognized rating agency will be able to sell their _____ at a reasonable price.
    a. Commercial paper
    b. Financial distress
    c. Book building
    d. Trade-off theory

16. A '_____' is a 'Charge' that is paid to obtain the right to delay a payment. Essentially, the payer purchases the right to make a given payment in the future instead of in the Present. The '_____', or 'Charge' that must be paid to delay the payment, is simply the difference between what the payment amount would be if it were paid in the present and what the payment amount would be paid if it were paid in the future.
    a. Risk modeling
    b. Value at risk
    c. Risk aversion
    d. Discount

17. _____ is a fee paid on borrowed assets. It is the price paid for the use of borrowed money, or, money earned by deposited funds. Assets that are sometimes lent with _____ include money, shares, consumer goods through hire purchase, major assets such as aircraft, and even entire factories in finance lease arrangements.
    a. A Random Walk Down Wall Street
    b. Insolvency
    c. AAB
    d. Interest

18. In accounting the prefix _____ is used adjectively to simply describe accounts that accrue interest. In contrast the term non-_____ is used to describe accounts that do not accrue interest.
    a. A Random Walk Down Wall Street
    b. ABN Amro
    c. Interest bearing
    d. AAB

19. A _____ is a fungible, negotiable instrument representing financial value. They are broadly categorized into debt securities (such as banknotes, bonds and debentures), and equity securities; e.g., common stocks. The company or other entity issuing the _____ is called the issuer.
    a. Securities lending
    b. Security
    c. Book entry
    d. Tracking stock

20. The U.S. _____ is an independent agency of the United States government which holds primary responsibility for enforcing the federal securities laws and regulating the securities industry, the nation's stock and options exchanges, and other electronic securities markets. The SEC was created by section 4 of the SEC of 1934 (now codified as 15 U.S.C. Â§ 78d and commonly referred to as the 1934 Act.)
    a. 7-Eleven
    b. Securities and Exchange Commission
    c. 529 plan
    d. 4-4-5 Calendar

21. An _____ is a loan, often for a short term, secured by a company's assets. Real estate, A/R, inventory, and equipment are typical assets used to back the loan. The loan may be backed by a single category of assets or some combination of assets, for instance, a combination of A/R and equipment.
    a. Asset-based loan
    b. ASCOT
    c. Amortizing loan
    d. External financing

Chapter 16. Short-Term Financing

22. _____ is a financial transaction whereby a business sells its accounts receivable (i.e., invoices) at a discount. _____ differs from a bank loan in three main ways. First, the emphasis is on the value of the receivables (essentially a financial asset), not the firm's credit worthiness.
- a. Debt-for-equity swap
- b. Financial Literacy Month
- c. Factoring
- d. Credit card balance transfer

23. _____ is a list for goods and materials held available in stock by a business. It is also used for a list of the contents of a household and for a list for testamentary purposes of the possessions of someone who has died. In accounting _____ is considered an asset.
- a. A Random Walk Down Wall Street
- b. ABN Amro
- c. Inventory
- d. AAB

24. A _____ is a property interest created by agreement or by operation of law over assets to secure the performance of an obligation, usually the payment of a debt. It gives the beneficiary of the _____ certain preferential rights in the disposition of secured assets. Such rights vary according to the type of _____, but in most cases, a holder of the _____ is entitled to seize, and usually sell, the property to discharge the debt that the _____ secures.
- a. Retention ratio
- b. Security interest
- c. Netting
- d. FIDC

25. In law, a _____ is a form of security interest granted over an item of property to secure the payment of a debt or performance of some other obligation. The owner of the property, who grants the _____, is referred to as the lienor and the person who has the benefit of the _____ is referred to as the _____ee.

The etymological root is: Anglo-French _____, loyen bond, restraint, from Latin ligamen, from ligare to bind.

- a. Sarbanes-Oxley Act
- b. Joint venture
- c. Family and Medical Leave Act
- d. Lien

26. _____ is a structured finance process that involves pooling and repackaging of cash-flow-producing financial assets into securities, which are then sold to investors. The term '_____' is derived from the fact that the form of financial instruments used to obtain funds from the investors are securities. As a portfolio risk backed by amortizing cash flows - and unlike general corporate debt - the credit quality of securitized debt is non-stationary due to changes in volatility that are time- and structure-dependent.
- a. Reputational risk
- b. The Glass-Steagall Act of 1933
- c. Securitization
- d. Special journals

27. The _____, effective annual interest rate, Annual Equivalent Rate (AER) or simply effective rate is the interest rate on a loan or financial product restated from the nominal interest rate as an interest rate with annual compound interest. It is used to compare the annual interest between loans with different compounding terms (daily, monthly, annually, or other.)

Chapter 16. Short-Term Financing

The _____ differs in two important respects from the annual percentage rate (APR):

1. the _____ generally does not incorporate one-time charges such as front-end fees;
2. the _____ is (generally) not defined by legal or regulatory authorities (as APR is in many jurisdictions.)

By contrast, the 'effective APR' is used as a legal term, where front-fees and other costs can be included, as defined by local law.

Annual Percentage Yield or effective annual yield is the analogous concept used for savings or investment products, such as a certificate of deposit.

    a. A Random Walk Down Wall Street   b. AAB
    c. ABN Amro   d. Effective interest rate

28. An _____ is the price a borrower pays for the use of money they do not own, and the return a lender receives for deferring the use of funds, by lending it to the borrower. _____s are normally expressed as a percentage rate over the period of one year.

_____s targets are also a vital tool of monetary policy and are used to control variables like investment, inflation, and unemployment.

    a. ABN Amro   b. A Random Walk Down Wall Street
    c. Interest rate   d. AAB

29. In economics, business, and accounting, a _____ is the value of money that has been used up to produce something, and hence is not available for use anymore. In business, the _____ may be one of acquisition, in which case the amount of money expended to acquire it is counted as _____. In this case, money is the input that is gone in order to acquire the thing.

    a. Sliding scale fees   b. Fixed costs
    c. Marginal cost   d. Cost

30. _____ are direct outlays of cash which may or may not be later reimbursed.

In operating a vehicle, gasoline, parking fees and tolls are considered _____ for the trip. Insurance, oil changes, and interest are not, because the outlay of cash covers expenses accrued over a longer period of time.

    a. ABN Amro   b. AAB
    c. A Random Walk Down Wall Street   d. Out-of-pocket expenses

31. In the United States, _____ is the function of offering loans to businesses. Commercial financing is generally offered by a bank or other lender. Most commercial banks offer commercial financing, and the loans are either secured by business assets or alternatively can be unsecured, where the lender relies of the cash flows of the business to repay the facility.

a. Normative economics
c. Bonus share
b. Volatility clustering
d. Commercial Finance

32. _____ is one of the largest professional services firms in the world. _____ employs over 123,000 people in a global network of member firms spanning over 145 countries. Composite revenues of _____ member firms in 2007 were $19.8 billion USD (17.4% growth from 2006.)

a. National Association of State Boards of Accountancy
c. KPMG
b. Texas ratio
d. Federal Deposit Insurance Corporation

33. The _____ is an expected return that the provider of capital plans to earn on their investment.

Capital (money) used for funding a business should earn returns for the capital providers who risk their capital. For an investment to be worthwhile, the expected return on capital must be greater than the _____.

a. Capital intensity
c. Weighted average cost of capital
b. 4-4-5 Calendar
d. Cost of capital

Chapter 17. Managing Multinational Cash Flows

1. In finance, the _____ between two currencies specifies how much one currency is worth in terms of the other. For example an _____ of 102 Japanese yen to the United States dollar means that JPY 102 is worth the same as USD 1. The foreign exchange market is one of the largest markets in the world.
   a. Exchange rate
   b. ABN Amro
   c. A Random Walk Down Wall Street
   d. AAB

2. The _____ of monetary management established the rules for commercial and financial relations among the world's major industrial states in the mid 20th Century. The _____ was the first example of a fully negotiated monetary order intended to govern monetary relations among independent nation-states.

   Preparing to rebuild the international economic system as World War II was still raging, 730 delegates from all 44 Allied nations gathered at the Mount Washington Hotel in Bretton Woods, New Hampshire, United States, for the United Nations Monetary and Financial Conference.

   a. Cash budget
   b. The Hong Kong Securities Institute
   c. Bretton Woods System
   d. Fixed Asset Register

3. A _____, sometimes called a pegged exchange rate, is a type of exchange rate regime wherein a currency's value is matched to the value of another single currency or to a basket of other currencies, or to another measure of value such as gold.

   A _____ is usually used to stabilize the value of a currency, vis-a-vis the currency it is pegged to. This facilitates trade and investments between the two countries, and is especially useful for small economies where external trade forms a large part of their GDP.

   a. Fixed exchange rate
   b. Deflation
   c. Market structure
   d. Human capital

4. A _____ or a flexible exchange rate is a type of exchange rate regime wherein a currency's value is allowed to fluctuate according to the foreign exchange market. A currency that uses a _____ is known as a floating currency. The opposite of a _____ is a fixed exchange rate.
   a. Spot market
   b. Currency pair
   c. Foreign exchange market
   d. Floating Exchange rate

5. _____ was an arrangement established in 1979 under the Jenkins European Commission where most nations of the European Economic Community (EEC) linked their currencies to prevent large fluctuations relative to one another.

   After the collapse of the Bretton Woods system in 1971, most of the EEC countries agreed in 1972 to maintain stable exchange rates by preventing exchange fluctuations of more than 2.25% (the European 'currency snake'.) In March 1979, this system was replaced by the _____, and the European Currency Unit (ECU) was defined.

   a. A Random Walk Down Wall Street
   b. European Monetary System
   c. Euro Interbank Offered Rate
   d. Exchange Rate Mechanism

6. A _____ secures the proper functioning of money by regulating economic agents, transaction types, and money supply.

They are traditionally formed by the policy decisions of individual governments and administrated as a domestic economic issue.

The current trend, however, is to use international trade and investment to alter the policy and legislation of individual governments.

a. Pattern day trader
b. Bond credit rating
c. Payback period
d. Monetary System

7. A _____ is an agreement between two parties to buy or sell an asset at a specified point of time in the future. The price of the underlying instrument, in whatever form, is paid before control of the instrument changes. This is one of the many forms of buy/sell orders where the time of trade is not the time where the securities themselves are exchanged.

a. Loan Credit Default Swap Index
b. Constant maturity credit default swap
c. Derivatives markets
d. Forward contract

8. In finance, a _____ is a standardized contract, to buy or sell a specified commodity of standardized quality at a certain date in the future, at a market determined price (the futures price.)

The price is determined by the instantaneous equilibrium between the forces of supply and demand among competing buy and sell orders on the exchange at the time of the purchase or sale of the contract.

In many cases, the items may be such non-traditional 'commodities' as foreign currencies, commercial or government paper [e.g., bonds], or 'baskets' of corporate equity ['stock indices'] or other financial instruments.

a. Repurchase agreement
b. Financial future
c. Heston model
d. Futures contract

9. _____ is a fee paid on borrowed assets. It is the price paid for the use of borrowed money , or, money earned by deposited funds . Assets that are sometimes lent with _____ include money, shares, consumer goods through hire purchase, major assets such as aircraft, and even entire factories in finance lease arrangements.

a. Insolvency
b. Interest
c. AAB
d. A Random Walk Down Wall Street

10. An _____ is the price a borrower pays for the use of money they do not own, and the return a lender receives for deferring the use of funds, by lending it to the borrower. _____s are normally expressed as a percentage rate over the period of one year.

_____s targets are also a vital tool of monetary policy and are used to control variables like investment, inflation, and unemployment.

a. Interest rate
b. ABN Amro
c. A Random Walk Down Wall Street
d. AAB

Chapter 17. Managing Multinational Cash Flows

11. In finance, a _____ is collateral that the holder of a position in securities, options, or futures contracts has to deposit to cover the credit risk of his counterparty (most often his broker.) This risk can arise if the holder has done any of the following:

- borrowed cash from the counterparty to buy securities or options,
- sold securities or options short, or
- entered into a futures contract.

The collateral can be in the form of cash or securities, and it is deposited in a _____ account. On U.S. futures exchanges, '_____' was formally called performance bond.

_____ buying is buying securities with cash borrowed from a broker, using other securities as collateral.

a. Margin
b. Credit
c. Procter ' Gamble
d. Share

12. _____ refers to a business or organization attempting to acquire goods or services to accomplish the goals of the enterprise. Though there are several organizations that attempt to set standards in the _____ process, processes can vary greatly between organizations. Typically the word '_____' is not used interchangeably with the word 'procurement', since procurement typically includes Expediting, Supplier Quality, and Traffic and Logistics (T'L) in addition to _____.

a. 7-Eleven
b. 4-4-5 Calendar
c. 529 plan
d. Purchasing

13. A _____ is an exchange of promises between two or more parties to do an act which is enforceable in a court of law. It is where an unqualified offer meets a qualified acceptance and the parties reach Consensus ad Idem. The parties must have the necessary capacity to _____ and the _____ must not be either trifling, indeterminate, impossible or illegal.

a. 4-4-5 Calendar
b. Contract
c. 7-Eleven
d. 529 plan

14. A _____ is a central financial exchange where people can trade standardized futures contracts; that is, a contract to buy specific quantities of a commodity or financial instrument at a specified price with delivery set at a specified time in the future.

Though the origins of futures trading can supposedly be traced to Ancient Greek or Phoenician times, the first modern organized _____ began in 1710 at the Dojima Rice Exchange in Osaka, Japan.

The United States followed in the early 1800s.

a. 4-4-5 Calendar
b. Futures Exchange
c. 7-Eleven
d. 529 plan

Chapter 17. Managing Multinational Cash Flows

15. The institution most often referenced by the word '_____' is a public or publicly traded _____, the shares of which are traded on a public stock exchange (e.g., the New York Stock Exchange or Nasdaq in the United States) where shares of stock of _____s are bought and sold by and to the general public. Most of the largest businesses in the world are publicly traded _____s. However, the majority of _____s are said to be closely held, privately held or close _____s, meaning that no ready market exists for the trading of shares.

   a. Federal Home Loan Mortgage Corporation   b. Depository Trust Company
   c. Protect   d. Corporation

16. _____ is the field of accountancy concerned with the preparation of financial statements for decision makers, such as stockholders, suppliers, banks, employees, government agencies, owners, and other stakeholders. The fundamental need for _____ is to reduce principal-agent problem by measuring and monitoring agents' performance and reporting the results to interested users.

_____ is used to prepare accounting information for people outside the organization or not involved in the day to day running of the company.

   a. 4-4-5 Calendar   b. Financial Accounting
   c. 7-Eleven   d. 529 plan

17. _____ is a measure of the ability of a debtor to pay their debts as and when they fall due. It is usually expressed as a ratio or a percentage of current liabilities.

For a corporation with a published balance sheet there are various ratios used to calculate a measure of liquidity.

   a. Operating profit margin   b. Accounting liquidity
   c. Operating leverage   d. Invested capital

18. In general, _____ means to allow a positive value and a negative value to set-off and partially or entirely cancel each other out.

In the context of credit risk, there are at least three specific types of _____:

- Close-out _____

- _____ by novation

- Settlement or payment _____

_____ decreases credit exposure, increases business with existing counterparties, and reduces both operational and settlement risk and operational costs.

   a. Forward price   b. Moneylender
   c. Netting   d. Reinvestment risk

19. _____ is a legally enforceable arrangement between a bank and a counterparty that creates a single legal obligation covering all included individual contracts. This means that a bank'e;s obligation, in the event of the default or insolvency of one of the parties, would be the net sum of all positive and negative fair values of contracts included in the _____ arrangement.
   a. 4-4-5 Calendar
   b. Deposit account
   c. Contractum trinius
   d. Bilateral netting

20. In banking and finance, _____ denotes all activities from the time a commitment is made for a transaction until it is settled. _____ is necessary because the speed of trades is much faster than the cycle time for completing the underlying transaction.

In its widest sense _____ involves the management of post-trading, pre-settlement credit exposures, to ensure that trades are settled in accordance with market rules, even if a buyer or seller should become insolvent prior to settlement.

   a. Share
   b. Procter ' Gamble
   c. Clearing house
   d. Clearing

21. _____ is a type of bank account where the money in the account is legally able to be withdrawn immediately upon demand (or 'at call'.) This type of bank account can also be referred to as a 'cheque' or 'checking' or transactional account.

This type of bank account, allowing immediate conversion of the account balance into cash or withdrawal to another account, can be contrasted with a time deposit (also known as a certificate of deposit or term deposit), where the funds are not legally available for immediate withdrawal by the depositor.

   a. 4-4-5 Calendar
   b. 529 plan
   c. Synthetic lease
   d. Demand deposit

22. In United States banking, _____ is a marketing term for certain services offered primarily to larger business customers. It may be used to describe all bank accounts (such as checking accounts) provided to businesses of a certain size, but it is more often used to describe specific services such as cash concentration, zero balance accounting, and automated clearing house facilities. Sometimes, private banking customers are given _____ services.
   a. Capitalization rate
   b. Global tactical asset allocation
   c. Profitability index
   d. Cash management

23. _____ is an event or condition under the contract between a buyer and a seller to exchange an asset for payment. In accounting, it is recognized by an entry in the books of account. It involves a change in the status of the finances of two or more businesses or individuals.
   a. Nominal value
   b. Tax shield
   c. Negative gearing
   d. Financial Transaction

Chapter 18. Managing Financial Risk With Derivatives

1. _____ is a fee paid on borrowed assets. It is the price paid for the use of borrowed money, or, money earned by deposited funds. Assets that are sometimes lent with _____ include money, shares, consumer goods through hire purchase, major assets such as aircraft, and even entire factories in finance lease arrangements.
   - a. Interest
   - b. Insolvency
   - c. AAB
   - d. A Random Walk Down Wall Street

2. An _____ is the price a borrower pays for the use of money they do not own, and the return a lender receives for deferring the use of funds, by lending it to the borrower. _____s are normally expressed as a percentage rate over the period of one year.

   _____s targets are also a vital tool of monetary policy and are used to control variables like investment, inflation, and unemployment.

   - a. ABN Amro
   - b. A Random Walk Down Wall Street
   - c. AAB
   - d. Interest rate

3. A _____ is a futures contract on a short term interest rate (STIR.) Contracts vary, but are often defined on an interest rate index such as 3-month sterling or US dollar LIBOR.

   They are traded across a wide range of currencies, including the G12 country currencies and many others.

   - a. Financial future
   - b. Notional amount
   - c. Real estate derivatives
   - d. Dual currency deposit

4. In finance, a _____ is a standardized contract, to buy or sell a specified commodity of standardized quality at a certain date in the future, at a market determined price (the futures price.)

   The price is determined by the instantaneous equilibrium between the forces of supply and demand among competing buy and sell orders on the exchange at the time of the purchase or sale of the contract.

   In many cases, the items may be such non-traditional 'commodities' as foreign currencies, commercial or government paper [e.g., bonds], or 'baskets' of corporate equity ['stock indices'] or other financial instruments.

   - a. Repurchase agreement
   - b. Financial future
   - c. Heston model
   - d. Futures contract

5. In finance, a _____ is a position established in one market in an attempt to offset exposure to the price risk of an equal but opposite obligation or position in another market -- usually, but not always, in the context of one's commercial activity. Hedging is a strategy designed to minimize exposure to such business risks as a sharp contraction in demand for one's inventory, while still allowing the business to profit from producing and maintaining that inventory. A typical hedger might be a farmer with 2000 acres of unharvested wheat in the ground, who would rather tend his crop without the distraction of uncertain prices.
   - a. 7-Eleven
   - b. 4-4-5 Calendar
   - c. 529 plan
   - d. Hedge

Chapter 18. Managing Financial Risk With Derivatives

6. In finance, a _____ is collateral that the holder of a position in securities, options, or futures contracts has to deposit to cover the credit risk of his counterparty (most often his broker.) This risk can arise if the holder has done any of the following:

- borrowed cash from the counterparty to buy securities or options,
- sold securities or options short, or
- entered into a futures contract.

The collateral can be in the form of cash or securities, and it is deposited in a _____ account. On U.S. futures exchanges, '_____' was formally called performance bond.

_____ buying is buying securities with cash borrowed from a broker, using other securities as collateral.

a. Procter ' Gamble
c. Credit
b. Margin
d. Share

7. The collateral can be in the form of cash or securities, and it is deposited in a _____. On U.S. futures exchanges, 'margin' was formally called performance bond.

Margin buying is buying securities with cash borrowed from a broker, using other securities as collateral.

a. Risk-neutral measure
c. Dollar roll
b. Margin account
d. Forward contract

8. In finance, the _____ is the global financial market for short-term borrowing and lending. It provides short-term liquidity funding for the global financial system. The _____ is where short-term obligations such as Treasury bills, commercial paper and bankers' acceptances are bought and sold.

a. Cramdown
c. Consumer debt
b. Money Market
d. Debt-for-equity swap

9. _____, in bookkeeping, refers to assets, liabilities, income, and expenses recorded on individual pages of the so called book of final entry or ledger. Changes in _____ value are made by chronologically posting debit (DR) and credit (CR) entries to its page. Examples of _____s are cash, _____s receivable, mortgages, loans, land and buildings, common stock, sales, services provided, wages, and payroll overhead.

a. Accretion
c. Alpha
b. Account
d. Option

10. A _____ is an exchange of promises between two or more parties to do an act which is enforceable in a court of law. It is where an unqualified offer meets a qualified acceptance and the parties reach Consensus ad Idem. The parties must have the necessary capacity to _____ and the _____ must not be either trifling, indeterminate, impossible or illegal.

a. 529 plan
c. 7-Eleven
b. 4-4-5 Calendar
d. Contract

11. The _____ is an American financial and commodity derivative exchange based in Chicago. The _____ was founded in 1898 as the Chicago Butter and Egg Board. Originally, the exchange was a non-profit organization.

Chapter 18. Managing Financial Risk With Derivatives

a. Gamelan Council
c. Financial Crimes Enforcement Network
b. Chicago Mercantile Exchange
d. Public Company Accounting Oversight Board

12. The _____ is a U.S. government-owned corporation within the Department of Housing and Urban Development

Ginnie Mae provides guarantees on mortgage-backed securities backed by federally insured or guaranteed loans, mainly loans issued by the Federal Housing Administration, Department of Veterans Affairs, Rural Housing Service, and Office of Public and Indian Housing. Ginnie Mae securities are the only MBS that are guaranteed by the United States government.

a. 4-4-5 Calendar
c. Graduated payment mortgage
b. Government National Mortgage Association
d. Jumbo mortgage

13. The variation margin or _____ is not collateral, but a daily offsetting of profits and losses. Futures are marked-to-market every day, so the current price is compared to the previous day's price. The profit or loss on the day of a position is then paid to or debited from the holder by the futures exchange.

a. Total return swap
c. Delivery month
b. SPI 200 futures contract
d. Maintenance margin

14. A _____, also FX future or foreign exchange future, is a futures contract to exchange one currency for another at a specified date in the future at a price (exchange rate) that is fixed on the purchase date. Typically, one of the currencies is the US dollar. The price of a future is then in terms of US dollars per unit of other currency.

a. Currency Future
c. Non-deliverable forward
b. Foreign exchange controls
d. Currency swap

15. A _____ is a financial contract between two parties, the buyer and the seller of this type of option. Often it is simply labeled a 'call'. The buyer of the option has the right, but not the obligation to buy an agreed quantity of a particular commodity or financial instrument (the underlying instrument) from the seller of the option at a certain time (the expiration date) for a certain price (the strike price.)

a. Bear call spread
c. Bear spread
b. Bull spread
d. Call option

16. An _____ is a contract written by a seller that conveys to the buyer the right -- but not the obligation -- to buy (in the case of a call _____) or to sell (in the case of a put _____) a particular asset, such as a piece of property such as, among others, a futures contract. In return for granting the _____, the seller collects a payment (the premium) from the buyer.

For example, buying a call _____ provides the right to buy a specified quantity of a security at a set strike price at some time on or before expiration, while buying a put _____ provides the right to sell.

a. Amortization
c. AT'T Mobility LLC
b. Annuity
d. Option

17. An _____ is defined as 'a promise which meets the requirements for the formation of a contract and limits the promisor's power to revoke an offer.' Restatement (Second) of Contracts § 25 (1981.)

Chapter 18. Managing Financial Risk With Derivatives

Quite simply, an _____ is a type of contract that protects an offeree from an offeror's ability to revoke the contract.

Consideration for the _____ is still required as it is still a form of contract.

a. A Random Walk Down Wall Street
c. ABN Amro
b. AAB
d. Option contract

18. A _____ is a financial contract between two parties, the seller (writer) and the buyer of the option. The put allows its buyer the right but not the obligation to sell a commodity or financial instrument (the underlying instrument) to the writer (seller) of the option at a certain time for a certain price (the strike price.) The writer (seller) has the obligation to purchase the underlying asset at that strike price, if the buyer exercises the option.

a. Bear call spread
c. Debit spread
b. Bear spread
d. Put option

19. _____ is a derivative financial instrument.

The global market for exchange-traded _____s is notionally valued by the Bank for International Settlements at $3,075,400 million in 2005.

a. Eurobond
c. Economic entity
b. Interest rate option
d. Education production function

20. The _____ (or notional principal amount or notional value) on a financial instrument is the nominal or face amount that is used to calculate payments made on that instrument. This amount generally does not change hands and is thus referred to as notional.

Contrast a bond with an interest rate swap:

- In a bond, the buyer pays the principal amount at issue (start), then receives coupons (computed off this principal) over the life of the bond, then receives the principal back at maturity (end.)
- In a swap, no principal changes hands at inception (start) or expiry (end), and in the meantime, interest payments are computed based on a _____, which acts as if it were the principal of a bond, hence the term notional principal amount, abbreviated to notional.

In simple terms the notional principal amount is essentially how much of the asset or bonds a person has. For example, if I bought a premium bond for £1 then the notional principal amount would be £1. Hence the notional principal amount is the quantity of the assets and bonds.

a. Forward start option
c. Basis trading
b. Credit derivative
d. Notional amount

21. In finance, a _____ is a derivative in which two counterparties agree to exchange one stream of cash flows against another stream. These streams are called the legs of the _____.

Chapter 18. Managing Financial Risk With Derivatives

The cash flows are calculated over a notional principal amount, which is usually not exchanged between counterparties.

a. Volatility arbitrage
b. Volatility swap
c. Local volatility
d. Swap

22. In business and accounting, _____s are everything of value that is owned by a person or company. The balance sheet of a firm records the monetary value of the _____s owned by the firm. The two major _____ classes are tangible _____s and intangible _____s.
a. Accounts payable
b. EBITDA
c. Income
d. Asset

23. An _____ is an exchange of tangible assets for intangible assets or vice versa. Since it is a swap of assets, the procedure takes place on the active side of the balance sheet and has no impact on the latter in regards to volume. As an example, a company may sell equity and receive the value in cash thus increasing liquidity.
a. AAB
b. A Random Walk Down Wall Street
c. ABN Amro
d. Asset swap

24. In the most general sense, a _____ is anything that is a hindrance, or puts individuals at a disadvantage.

Before we discuss the financial terms, we should note that a _____ can also have a much more important slang meaning.

This is best described in an example.

a. Limited liability
b. McFadden Act
c. Covenant
d. Liability

25. In finance, the _____ between two currencies specifies how much one currency is worth in terms of the other. For example an _____ of 102 Japanese yen to the United States dollar means that JPY 102 is worth the same as USD 1. The foreign exchange market is one of the largest markets in the world.
a. AAB
b. A Random Walk Down Wall Street
c. ABN Amro
d. Exchange rate

26. A _____ is a financial contract whose value is derived from the value of something else (known as the underlying.) The underlying on which a _____ is based can be an asset, weather conditions bonds or other forms of credit.
a. 7-Eleven
b. 4-4-5 Calendar
c. 529 plan
d. Derivative

27. The role of the _____ is to issue accounting standards in the United Kingdom. It is recognised for that purpose under the Companies Act 1985. It took over the task of setting accounting standards from the Accounting Standards Committee (ASC) in 1990.

a. ABN Amro
b. AAB
c. A Random Walk Down Wall Street
d. Accounting Standards Board

28. The _____ founded on April 1, 2001 is the successor of the International Accounting Standards Committee (IASC) founded in June 1973 in London. It is responsible for developing the International Financial Reporting Standards (new name for the International Accounting Standards issued after 2001), and promoting the use and application of these standards.

The _____ is an independent, privately-funded accounting standard-setter based in London, UK.

a. Association of Certified Public Accountants
b. International Federation of Accountants
c. American Accounting Association
d. International Accounting Standards Board

29. _____ (or PwC) is one of the world's largest professional services firms. It was formed in 1998 from a merger between Price Waterhouse and Coopers ' Lybrand, both formed in London.

_____ earned aggregated worldwide revenues of $28 billion for fiscal 2008, and employed over 146,000 people in 150 countries.

a. Lending Club
b. Credit karma
c. Texas ratio
d. PricewaterhouseCoopers

Chapter 19. Treasury Information Management

1. A _____ is a pool of assets forming an independent legal entity that are bought with the contributions to a pension plan for the exclusive purpose of financing pension plan benefits.

   _____s are important shareholders of listed and private companies. They are especially important to the stock market where large institutional investors like the Ontario Teachers' Pension Plan dominate.

   a. Limited liability company
   b. Pension fund
   c. Leveraged buyout
   d. Leverage

2. _____ is the provision of resources (such as granting a loan) by one party to another party where that second party does not reimburse the first party immediately, thereby generating a debt, and instead arranges either to repay or return those resources (or material(s) of equal value) at a later date. The first party is called a creditor, also known as a lender, while the second party is called a debtor, also known as a borrower.

   Movements of financial capital are normally dependent on either _____ or equity transfers.

   a. Comparable
   b. Credit
   c. Warrant
   d. Clearing house

3. _____, consists of the buying and selling of products or services over electronic systems such as the Internet and other computer networks. The amount of trade conducted electronically has grown extraordinarily with widespread Internet usage. The use of commerce is conducted in this way, spurring and drawing on innovations in electronic funds transfer, supply chain management, Internet marketing, online transaction processing, electronic data interchange (EDI), inventory management systems, and automated data collection systems.
   a. AAB
   b. Electronic commerce
   c. A Random Walk Down Wall Street
   d. ABN Amro

4. In banking and finance, _____ denotes all activities from the time a commitment is made for a transaction until it is settled. _____ is necessary because the speed of trades is much faster than the cycle time for completing the underlying transaction.

   In its widest sense _____ involves the management of post-trading, pre-settlement credit exposures, to ensure that trades are settled in accordance with market rules, even if a buyer or seller should become insolvent prior to settlement.

   a. Share
   b. Procter ' Gamble
   c. Clearing house
   d. Clearing

5. In economics, business, and accounting, a _____ is the value of money that has been used up to produce something, and hence is not available for use anymore. In business, the _____ may be one of acquisition, in which case the amount of money expended to acquire it is counted as _____. In this case, money is the input that is gone in order to acquire the thing.
   a. Cost
   b. Fixed costs
   c. Sliding scale fees
   d. Marginal cost

6. _____ refers to the computer-based systems used to perform financial transactions electronically.

Chapter 19. Treasury Information Management

The term is used for a number of different concepts:

- Cardholder-initiated transactions, where a cardholder makes use of a payment card
- Direct deposit payroll payments for a business to its employees, possibly via a payroll services company
- Direct debit payments from customer to business, where the transaction is initiated by the business with customer permission
- Electronic bill payment in online banking, which may be delivered by _____ or paper check
- Transactions involving stored value of electronic money, possibly in a private currency
- Wire transfer via an international banking network (generally carries a higher fee)
- Electronic Benefit Transfer

Electronic funds transferPOS (short for _____ at Point of Sale) is an Australian and New Zealand electronic processing system for credit cards, debit cards and charge cards.

European banks and card companies also sometimes reference 'Electronic funds transferPOS' as the system used for processing card transactions through terminals on points of sale, though the system is not the trademarked Australian/New Zealand variant.

Credit cards

_____ may be initiated by a cardholder when a payment card such as a credit card or debit card is used.

a. A Random Walk Down Wall Street   b. AAB
c. ABN Amro   d. Electronic funds transfer

7. A _____ is a financial services company that provides clearing and settlement services for financial transactions, usually on a futures exchange, and often acts as central counterparty (the payor actually pays the _____, which then pays the payee). A _____ may also offer novation, the substitution of a new contract or debt for an old, or other credit enhancement services to its members.

The term is also used for banks like Suffolk Bank that acted as a restraint on the over-issuance of private bank notes.

a. Clearing House   b. Valuation
c. Warrant   d. Bucket shop

8. The institution most often referenced by the word '_____' is a public or publicly traded _____, the shares of which are traded on a public stock exchange (e.g., the New York Stock Exchange or Nasdaq in the United States) where shares of stock of _____s are bought and sold by and to the general public. Most of the largest businesses in the world are publicly traded _____s. However, the majority of _____s are said to be closely held, privately held or close _____s, meaning that no ready market exists for the trading of shares.

a. Federal Home Loan Mortgage Corporation   b. Corporation
c. Depository Trust Company   d. Protect

Chapter 19. Treasury Information Management

9. _____ is the discipline of identifying, monitoring and limiting risks. In some cases the acceptable risk may be near zero. Risks can come from accidents, natural causes and disasters as well as deliberate attacks from an adversary.
   a. FIFO
   b. Penny stock
   c. 4-4-5 Calendar
   d. Risk Management

10. In United States banking, _____ is a marketing term for certain services offered primarily to larger business customers. It may be used to describe all bank accounts (such as checking accounts) provided to businesses of a certain size, but it is more often used to describe specific services such as cash concentration, zero balance accounting, and automated clearing house facilities. Sometimes, private banking customers are given _____ services.
   a. Cash Management
   b. Profitability index
   c. Capitalization rate
   d. Global tactical asset allocation

11. Electronic Bill Presentment ' Payment (EBPP) is a form of electronic billing where a company bills its customers and receives payment electronically over the Internet. As the name also denotes, it addresses not only Bill Presentment, but also when applicable the process model for consumer payments to business.

    The _____ model was created by Council for Electronic Billing and Payment of the National Automated Clearing House Association.

   a. A Random Walk Down Wall Street
   b. ABN Amro
   c. AAB
   d. Electronic Bill Presentment & Payment

12. _____ is the level of inventory that minimizes the total inventory holding costs and ordering costs. The framework used to determine this order quantity is also known as Wilson _____ Model. The model was developed by F. W. Harris in 1913.
   a. AAB
   b. A Random Walk Down Wall Street
   c. ABN Amro
   d. Economic order quantity

13. _____ is one of the oldest financial services firms in the world. It is a leader in financial services with assets of $2.3 trillion., and the largest market capitalization and deposit base of any U.S. banking institution.
   a. Comanity
   b. Double-declining-balance method
   c. JPMorgan Chase ' Co.
   d. Weighted mean

14. _____, in bookkeeping, refers to assets, liabilities, income, and expenses recorded on individual pages of the so called book of final entry or ledger. Changes in _____ value are made by chronologically posting debit (DR) and credit (CR) entries to its page. Examples of _____s are cash, _____s receivable, mortgages, loans, land and buildings, common stock, sales, services provided, wages, and payroll overhead.
   a. Accretion
   b. Account
   c. Alpha
   d. Option

15. _____ is a file or account that contains money that a person or company owes to suppliers, but hasn't paid yet (a form of debt.) When you receive an invoice you add it to the file, and then you remove it when you pay. Thus, the A/P is a form of credit that suppliers offer to their purchasers by allowing them to pay for a product or service after it has already been received.

Chapter 19. Treasury Information Management

a. Accrual
b. Accounts payable
c. Earnings before interest, taxes, depreciation and amortization
d. Outstanding balance

16. _____ is the balance of the amounts of cash being received and paid by a business during a defined period of time, sometimes tied to a specific project. Measurement of _____ can be used

- to evaluate the state or performance of a business or project.
- to determine problems with liquidity. Being profitable does not necessarily mean being liquid. A company can fail because of a shortage of cash, even while profitable.
- to generate project rate of returns. The time of _____s into and out of projects are used as inputs to financial models such as internal rate of return, and net present value.
- to examine income or growth of a business when it is believed that accrual accounting concepts do not represent economic realities. Alternately, _____ can be used to 'validate' the net income generated by accrual accounting.

_____ as a generic term may be used differently depending on context, and certain _____ definitions may be adapted by analysts and users for their own uses. Common terms include operating _____ and free _____.

_____s can be classified into:

1. Operational _____s: Cash received or expended as a result of the company's core business activities.
2. Investment _____s: Cash received or expended through capital expenditure, investments or acquisitions.
3. Financing _____s: Cash received or expended as a result of financial activities, such as interests and dividends.

All three together - the net _____ - are necessary to reconcile the beginning cash balance to the ending cash balance. Loan draw downs or equity injections, that is just shifting of capital but no expenditure as such, are not considered in the net _____.

a. Real option
b. Corporate finance
c. Shareholder value
d. Cash flow

17. _____ refers to a business or organization attempting to acquire goods or services to accomplish the goals of the enterprise. Though there are several organizations that attempt to set standards in the _____ process, processes can vary greatly between organizations. Typically the word '_____' is not used interchangeably with the word 'procurement', since procurement typically includes Expediting, Supplier Quality, and Traffic and Logistics (T'L) in addition to _____.

a. 7-Eleven
b. 529 plan
c. 4-4-5 Calendar
d. Purchasing

18. _____ is a list for goods and materials held available in stock by a business. It is also used for a list of the contents of a household and for a list for testamentary purposes of the possessions of someone who has died. In accounting _____ is considered an asset.

Chapter 19. Treasury Information Management

a. ABN Amro
c. AAB
b. A Random Walk Down Wall Street
d. Inventory

19. The _____ of 2002 (Pub.L. 107-204, 116 Stat. 745, enacted July 30, 2002), also known as the Public Company Accounting Reform and Investor Protection Act of 2002 and commonly called Sarbanes-Oxley, Sarbox or SOX, is a United States federal law enacted on July 30, 2002 in response to a number of major corporate and accounting scandals including those affecting Enron, Tyco International, Adelphia, Peregrine Systems and WorldCom.
   a. Foreign Corrupt Practices Act
   c. Duty of loyalty
   b. Blue sky law
   d. Sarbanes-Oxley Act

20. _____ is the concept of adding accumulated interest back to the principal, so that interest is earned on interest from that moment on. The act of declaring interest to be principal is called compounding (i.e., interest is compounded.) A loan, for example, may have its interest compounded every month: in this case, a loan with $100 principal and 1% interest per month would have a balance of $101 at the end of the first month.
   a. Penny stock
   c. Compound interest
   b. 4-4-5 Calendar
   d. Risk management

21. In finance, the _____ approach describes a method of valuing a project, company, or asset using the concepts of the time value of money. All future cash flows are estimated and discounted to give their present values. The discount rate used is generally the appropriate cost of capital and may incorporate judgments of the uncertainty (riskiness) of the future cash flows.
   a. Present value of benefits
   c. Future-oriented
   b. Discounted cash flow
   d. Net present value

22. A '_____' is a 'Charge' that is paid to obtain the right to delay a payment. Essentially, the payer purchases the right to make a given payment in the future instead of in the Present. The '_____', or 'Charge' that must be paid to delay the payment, is simply the difference between what the payment amount would be if it were paid in the present and what the payment amount would be paid if it were paid in the future.
   a. Risk aversion
   c. Value at risk
   b. Discount
   d. Risk modeling

23. The _____, effective annual interest rate, Annual Equivalent Rate (AER) or simply effective rate is the interest rate on a loan or financial product restated from the nominal interest rate as an interest rate with annual compound interest. It is used to compare the annual interest between loans with different compounding terms (daily, monthly, annually, or other.)

The _____ differs in two important respects from the annual percentage rate (APR):

1. the _____ generally does not incorporate one-time charges such as front-end fees;
2. the _____ is (generally) not defined by legal or regulatory authorities (as APR is in many jurisdictions.)

By contrast, the 'effective APR' is used as a legal term, where front-fees and other costs can be included, as defined by local law.

Annual Percentage Yield or effective annual yield is the analogous concept used for savings or investment products, such as a certificate of deposit.

a. A Random Walk Down Wall Street
c. ABN Amro
b. AAB
d. Effective interest rate

24. _____ is a fee paid on borrowed assets. It is the price paid for the use of borrowed money, or, money earned by deposited funds. Assets that are sometimes lent with _____ include money, shares, consumer goods through hire purchase, major assets such as aircraft, and even entire factories in finance lease arrangements.
   a. AAB
   b. Interest
   c. Insolvency
   d. A Random Walk Down Wall Street

25. In finance, the value of an option consists of two components, its intrinsic value and its _____. Time value is simply the difference between option value and intrinsic value. _____ is also known as theta, extrinsic value, or instrumental value.
   a. Debt buyer
   b. Conservatism
   c. Global Squeeze
   d. Time value

26. Simply put, _____ is the value of money figuring in a given amount of interest for a given amount of time. For example 100 dollars of todays money held for a year at 5 percent interest is worth 105 dollars, therefore 100 dollars paid now or 105 dollars paid exactly one year from now is the same amount of payment of money with that given intersest at that given amount of time. This notion dates at least to Martín de Azpilcueta of the School of Salamanca.

All of the standard calculations for _____ derive from the most basic algebraic expression for the present value of a future sum, 'discounted' to the present by an amount equal to the _____. For example, a sum of FV to be received in one year is discounted (at the rate of interest r) to give a sum of PV at present: PV = FV -- rÂ·PV = FV/(1+r).

   a. Current account
   b. Zero-coupon bond
   c. Coefficient of variation
   d. Time value of money

27. An _____ can be defined as a contract which provides an income stream in return for an initial payment.

An immediate _____ is an _____ for which the time between the contract date and the date of the first payment is not longer than the time interval between payments. A common use for an immediate _____ is to provide a pension to a retired person or persons.

   a. AT'T Inc.
   b. Annuity
   c. Intrinsic value
   d. Amortization

28. _____ or net present worth (NPW) is defined as the total present value (PV) of a time series of cash flows. It is a standard method for using the time value of money to appraise long-term projects. Used for capital budgeting, and widely throughout economics, it measures the excess or shortfall of cash flows, in present value terms, once financing charges are met.
   a. Net present value
   b. Negative gearing
   c. Tax shield
   d. Present value of costs

Chapter 19. Treasury Information Management

29. A _____ is an annuity in which the periodic payments begin on a fixed date and continue indefinitely. It is sometimes referred to as a perpetual annuity. Fixed coupon payments on permanently invested (irredeemable) sums of money are prime examples of these. Scholarships paid perpetually from an endowment fit the definition of _____.

    a. Perpetuity
    b. LIBOR market model
    c. Current yield
    d. Stochastic volatility

30. _____ is the value on a given date of a future payment or series of future payments, discounted to reflect the time value of money and other factors such as investment risk. _____ calculations are widely used in business and economics to provide a means to compare cash flows at different times on a meaningful 'like to like' basis.

    The most commonly applied model of the time value of money is compound interest.

    a. Net present value
    b. Present value of benefits
    c. Negative gearing
    d. Present value

31. _____ is the difference between price and the costs of bringing to market whatever it is that is accounted as an enterprise (whether by harvest, extraction, manufacture, or purchase) in terms of the component costs of delivered goods and/or services and any operating or other expenses.

    A key difficulty in measuring profit is in defining costs. Pure economic monetary profits can be zero or negative even in competitive equilibrium when accounted monetized costs exceed monetized price.

    a. A Random Walk Down Wall Street
    b. Accounting profit
    c. AAB
    d. Economic profit

Chapter 1
1. c 2. d 3. c 4. a 5. b 6. d 7. d 8. d 9. a 10. d
11. d 12. d 13. a 14. a 15. d

Chapter 2
1. b 2. b 3. d 4. a 5. c 6. d 7. c 8. d 9. a 10. d
11. d 12. d 13. a

Chapter 3
1. a 2. d 3. a 4. b 5. b 6. d 7. d 8. d 9. d 10. a
11. c 12. b 13. d 14. d 15. b 16. d 17. d 18. d 19. a 20. a
21. d 22. a 23. d 24. b 25. d

Chapter 4
1. b 2. b 3. d 4. d 5. d 6. a 7. d 8. d 9. c 10. c
11. d 12. a 13. d 14. d 15. a 16. b 17. c 18. d 19. a 20. d

Chapter 5
1. a 2. d 3. d 4. d 5. d 6. d 7. d 8. b 9. d 10. d
11. d 12. d 13. c 14. d 15. b

Chapter 6
1. d 2. c 3. c 4. d 5. a 6. c 7. b 8. d 9. d 10. d
11. d 12. d 13. d 14. a 15. d 16. d 17. d 18. b 19. c

Chapter 7
1. b 2. d 3. d 4. d 5. b 6. d 7. d 8. d 9. a 10. d
11. d 12. b

Chapter 8
1. b 2. b 3. d 4. d 5. b 6. a 7. b 8. d 9. c 10. d
11. b 12. a 13. d 14. c 15. d 16. c 17. d 18. a 19. d 20. a
21. a 22. b 23. a 24. a 25. d 26. b 27. b 28. c 29. d 30. b
31. d 32. b 33. a 34. c 35. c 36. d 37. d 38. d 39. d 40. b

Chapter 9
1. c 2. c 3. d 4. d 5. b 6. b 7. b 8. d 9. b 10. a
11. a 12. d

Chapter 10
1. c 2. a 3. b 4. b 5. a 6. d 7. a 8. a 9. b 10. a
11. d 12. d

Chapter 11
1. d 2. d 3. d 4. c 5. d 6. b 7. d 8. d 9. a 10. d
11. d 12. a 13. d 14. d 15. d 16. c 17. d 18. d 19. d

ANSWER KEY

Chapter 12
1. c   2. b   3. d   4. b   5. a   6. d   7. c   8. d   9. b   10. a
11. a   12. d   13. b   14. a   15. c   16. c   17. d   18. b   19. a   20. c
21. d   22. c   23. c   24. a   25. d   26. b   27. c   28. d

Chapter 13
1. b   2. c   3. d   4. d   5. d   6. d   7. a

Chapter 14
1. d   2. d   3. d   4. c   5. d   6. b   7. c   8. b   9. d   10. d
11. d   12. b   13. d   14. a   15. b   16. b   17. d   18. b   19. c   20. c
21. d   22. d   23. d   24. b   25. d   26. d   27. a   28. a   29. a   30. d
31. d   32. b   33. b   34. c   35. a   36. d   37. d   38. a   39. c   40. c
41. d   42. a   43. c   44. a   45. d   46. d

Chapter 15
1. d   2. a   3. a   4. d   5. d   6. c   7. d   8. b   9. a   10. a
11. d   12. d   13. d   14. a   15. b   16. d   17. a   18. b   19. a   20. c
21. a   22. d   23. a   24. d   25. d   26. d   27. d   28. d

Chapter 16
1. a   2. d   3. d   4. d   5. a   6. b   7. b   8. d   9. b   10. c
11. c   12. c   13. b   14. b   15. a   16. d   17. d   18. c   19. b   20. b
21. a   22. c   23. c   24. b   25. d   26. c   27. d   28. c   29. d   30. d
31. d   32. c   33. d

Chapter 17
1. a   2. c   3. a   4. d   5. b   6. d   7. d   8. d   9. b   10. a
11. a   12. d   13. b   14. b   15. d   16. b   17. b   18. c   19. d   20. d
21. d   22. d   23. d

Chapter 18
1. a   2. d   3. a   4. d   5. d   6. b   7. b   8. b   9. b   10. d
11. b   12. b   13. d   14. a   15. d   16. b   17. d   18. d   19. b   20. d
21. d   22. d   23. d   24. d   25. d   26. d   27. d   28. d   29. d

Chapter 19
1. b   2. b   3. b   4. d   5. a   6. d   7. a   8. b   9. d   10. a
11. d   12. d   13. c   14. b   15. b   16. d   17. d   18. d   19. d   20. c
21. b   22. b   23. d   24. b   25. d   26. d   27. b   28. a   29. a   30. d
31. b

www.ingramcontent.com/pod-product-compliance
Lightning Source LLC
Chambersburg PA
CBHW081846230426
43669CB00018B/2832